IMAGES OF WALES

SOUTH WALES COLLIERIES

VOLUME ONE

I SING OF WALES
MI GANAF GÂN

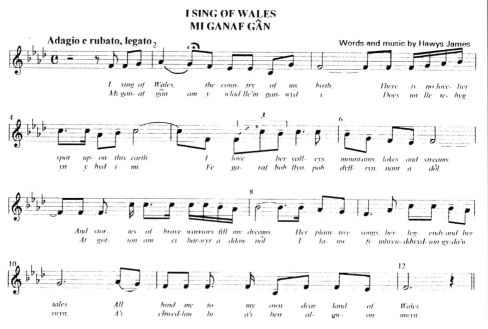

Words and music by Hawys James

I sing of Wales, where saints once walked the land,
I sing with joy of David and his band,
I read with pride of Wales' history,
Her poets and her writers bring to me
A treasure and a wealth of centuries past
My heritage, my birthright that will last.

Am Gymru canaf lle troediai'r saint di-ri.
Am Ddewi a'i ddilynwyr canaf i,
Â balchder darllenaf am ei hanes hen,
Trysorau mewn barddoniaeth a mewn llên -
Cyfraniad gwerthfawr o'r canrifoedd gynt -
Fy etifeddiaeth a'm treftadaeth ynt.

I sing of Wales where miners slaved for coal,
Explosions, falls and gas that took their toll,
Their pain and struggles, hardships, toil and sweat
Are sacrifices we must not forget,
Their sorrows borne with fortitude and pride
And for a paltry wage so many died.

Am Gymru canaf lle slafiodd glowyr hy'
Mewn tanchwa, cwymp a nwy mewn talcen du,
Eu llafur a'u chwys oedd uchel bris y glo,
A'u haberth mawr rhaid cadw byth mewn co',
A thynged llawer glöwr tlawd di-barch
Ar gyflog bitw oedd yr hers a'r arch.

IMAGES OF WALES

SOUTH WALES COLLIERIES
VOLUME ONE

DAVID OWEN

First published in 2001 by Tempus Publishing
Reprinted 2004

Reprinted in 2010 by
The History Press
The Mill, Brimscombe Port,
Stroud, Gloucestershire, GL5 2QG
www.thehistorypress.co.uk

Reprinted 2011

ISBN 978 0 7524 2364 7

Typesetting and origination by Tempus Publishing Limited
Printed and bound in Great Britain by
Marston Book Services Limited, Didcot

Acknowledgements

Thank you all for the wonderful stories, songs, poems, drawings and photographs of the South Wales Collieries, which have been given to me by the people from the mining villages of South Wales.

These have come from the early days of the coal industry through to the new millennium. I dedicate my book to the people of South Wales, the Land of Song, and in memory of all the miners who worked at the collieries.

I sincerely thank everyone for their kindness and help.

David Owen
Author and Archivist

Cydnabyddiaeth

Diolch am yr holl storïau, caneuon, cerddi, darluniau a ffotograffau aruthrol o Faes Glo De Cymru, sydd wedi eu cynnig i mi gan bobl pentrefi glofaol De Cymru.

Mae'r cyfraniadau yma yn dod o ddyddiau cynnar y diwydiant glo trwyddo i'r milflwydd newydd. Rwy'n cyflwyno'r llyfr yma i bobl Gwlad y Gân De Cymru er cof am y glowyr a wethiodd yn y pyllau glo.

Rwy'n diolch yn ddidwyll i bawb am eu caredigrwydd a cymorth.

David Owen
Awdur ac Archifydd

Contents

Preface

Mam. A debt that can never be repaid is owed to the miners of the South Wales Coalfield and a tribute should also be paid to their wives and families.

In the early 1800s women worked underground in the coalmines. Mother and child often worked together dragging drams of coal along the dark, narrow tunnels. The mother would have a belt around her waist and a chain between her legs attached to the dram and she would haul the dram-load of coal on all fours. As there were no water pumps at that time, there were pools of water on the pit-floor so her clothes would be wet all day. She'd carry on working even when pregnant. Women continued to work as surface workers until the 1920s.

The mother, 'Mam', was the pivot around whom the family revolved and her life revolved around her family. It was taken for granted that, like her collier husband, she was 'married' to the pit and she became accustomed to a life laden with hardships and sorrows without hardly ever complaining. This was her destiny and she accepted it, there was no option. She never knew whether her miner husband or sons would be involved in a pit accident and would be brought home dead or injured. Children, too, suffered from many illnesses- diphtheria, scarlet fever and tuberculosis were diseases that were rife. Infant mortality was high. Mothers had to be good nurses because many husbands became invalids through silicosis, pneumoconiosis and heart and chest complaints.

The family came first, they were mam's priorities and she was prepared to sacrifice everything, even to go without food herself to make sure that her husband and children had good, nourishing food. As a result, many mothers became anaemic and as there was no money for treatment, many died.

Mam was also Chancellor of the Exchequer and she looked after all the money that came into the house. She would go on marches and she played an important part in the strike and lock-outs. Women also organised the soup kitchens.

After the First World War the woman's role changed. During the war she had done a man's work in factories and arsenals and she wasn't prepared to be just a housewife any more. Many had full or part-time jobs, they went to pubs and clubs with their husbands, they had all the modern conveniences in the home. There were pit-head baths, no washing of dirty pit-clothes. During the 1984 strike the women organised food kitchens and collected money and food. They even went on picket duty. As in the past they supported their men but the archetypal miner's wife, 'Mam', had disappeared.

David Owen is to be congratulated on his first-rate and impressive collection of photographs in this book presenting a pictorial history of the South Wales Coalfield.

The struggles of the miners and their families time cannot erase and we extol their sacrifice and courage.

Hawys, composer, and Glyn James Hon Alderman and former Mayor of the Rhondda

Foreword

I am very honoured to have been asked to commend author David Owen on his dedication to recording the photographic history of some of the great Coal Mining Valleys that we have in South Wales.

I have been brought up in a mining village with a family that have suffered greatly because of the mining industry. My grandfather died of pneumoconiosis at the age of forty-four. My father and both by brothers also worked in the industry.

Having worked at the coalface at various South Wales Collieries I have personally experienced both the 'best and worst' scenarios within the industry. The memories that I have of mining are truly priceless because I know that the individuals who worked in the industry during my 'era', wherever they may have worked would have gone through very similar situations and experiences, hence leading to what I think is a bond between mining communities throughout the valleys.

Within this book I feel that David Owen has captured the true sentiments of the mining communities of the South Wales Coalfield.

Wayne Thomas
South Wales National Union of Mineworkers (NUM) General Secretary

Rhagair

Mae'n anrhydedd mawr cael eich gofyn i gymeradwyo ymrwymiad yr awdur, David Owen, a'i gofnod o hanes ffotograffig rhai o'r Cymoedd Glofaol mawr sydd gennym yn Ne Cymru.

Fe'm magwyd i mewn pentref glofaol gyda theulu oedd wedi dioddef cryn dipyn oherwydd y diwydiant glofaol. Bu farw fy nhad-cu o glefyd y llwch pan oedd yn 44 mlwydd oed. Fe weithiodd fy nhad a'i ddau frawd hefyd yn y diwydiant.

Wedi gweithio ar wyneb y graig mewn sawl pwll glo yn Ne Cymru, rydw i wedi profi'r 'gorau a'r gwaethaf' o fod o fewn y diwydiant. Mae fy atgofion o weithio yn y pyllau glo yn amhrisiadwy oherwydd rwy'n gwybod bod yr unigolion a weithiodd yn y diwydiant yn ystod fy nghyfnod i wedi mynd trwy brofiadau tebyg, sydd yn creu dealltwriaeth a theimlad o undod ymysg y cymunedau glofaol ar draws y cymoedd.

O fewn cloriau'r llyfr mae David Owen wedi crynhoi gwir ymdeimlad cymunedau glofaol Maes Glo De Cymru.

Wayne Thomas
Ysgrifennydd Cyffredinol Undeb Cenedlaethol Glowyr De Cymru

Introduction

Coal also known as the Black Diamond and Black Gold.
Found in the South Wales Valleys and Mountains of Old.
It doesn't Shine it Glitters with Peculiar Brilliance and Sparkle like Gold.

There are few substances in nature more unprepossessing in appearance than coal, few, gleaming with a ruddy light on winter eves that are more attractive. Similarly, if the theme has a hard, repellent look, let us see if it cannot be made interesting and have an instructive influence as well. Widespread in its location, coal may be assumed to have a place in the language of most nations. It is the *gahal* of the Hebrew, the *glo* of the old Briton, the *anthrax* of the Greek, the *carbo* of the Roman, the *coll* of the Saxon, the *kohle* of the Teuton and his Dutch and German descendant and the *charbon de terre* of that vivacious neighbour of ours opposite, the Frenchman.

There are twenty-eight references to coal in the Old and New Testaments and these show conclusively that its uses were as well known and as varied as now.

British historians generally concur in the opinion that coal was well known here before the arrival of the Romans and was used by workers in brass. The Britons knew coal by the primitive name of *glo* and the use of coal by the Romans in Wales was proved by an interesting discovery of a Roman villa near Caerleon.

In the thirteenth century coal was being turned out at Llanvabon, the monks of Neath and Margam were similarly employed and very likely used it for their temporal good. Another claim for ancient coal working is Swansea, the Norman lord, William de Breos, AD 1305, 'empowering the tenant to dig Pit coal at Byllywasted, without the hindrance of ourselves or heirs.'

In the centre of the old Norman castles of the thirteenth and fourteenth centuries stood the smithy who was our earliest ironmaster who used coal as well as charcoal in his labour at Morlais Castle.

The primitive mode of working in Elizabethan days was to drive a level and when they found the coal they worked holes, one for every digger, each miner working with candle light, they had boys that carried the coal in baskets on their backs to the entrance and they worked from 6:00a.m. to 6:00p.m. every day. These primitive operations did not extend much beyond the scratching of the surface and it was not until the closing decades of the eighteenth century that coal mining as a settled industry sprang into being in this area. This was due to the utilisation of coal for smelting iron, a development in which the first John Guest of Dowlais – the founder of a family destined to play a large part in the industrial and commercial life of Glamorgan – was a pioneer.

In the opening of the nineteenth century coal was worked on a considerable scale in the Merthyr and Dowlais areas, the output being in excess of the iron-smelting needs of the time and there are records of a proportion of that excess finding its way down to Cardiff and over mountain tracks into Herefordshire

Towards the middle of the nineteenth century a few far-seeing men, outside the coterie of ironmasters, apprehended the immense values connoted on the new term, 'South Wales Smokeless Steam Coal', a term which within a short period was to attain and establish a standard of coal value the whole world over and men set to work as pioneers in beginnings so humble and difficulties so immense that no one who reads the story of their work can with hold a tribute to their courage and their faith.

In this, the new stage of the development of the South Wales Coalfield, the Cynon Valley, was undoubtedly first. The production of coal in the Cynon Valley in 1844 was 71,031tons, in 1856 1,173,459tons and in 1870 2,342,792tons.

In the Rhondda Valley and Llantwit Fardre district coal output in these early days of development in 1856 was 205,200tons and in 1870 1,858,826tons.

One

The Cynon Valley in the South Wales Coalfield

If we could soar up with the eagle to an altitude commanding the Monmouthshire hills and the Pembrokeshire coast, the great field would be seen spread out before us, extending from Pontypool to Saint Bride's Bay, assumed by various authorities to be from seven hundred to a thousand square miles in length. Then looking more westwardly, we should be able to take on its extreme breadth of twenty-four miles from Dowlais to Llantrisant in Glamorgan and thus compass the whole.

This great field includes nearly the whole of Glamorgan and a huge slice of Monmouthshire; it further extends into the shires of Brecon, Carmarthen and Pembroke. The mass of the coalfield is covered by mountain and valley, by wood, pasture and river. Nine miles in length by two and a half miles in breadth are covered by the Swansea Bay, nine miles in length by five miles in width are covered by the estuary of Burry and the Llwchwr rivers and from Kidwelly the Carmarthen Bay covers an extent in length fifteen miles, with an average width of six miles.

So the journeyer, guided by the practical experience of the first describer of the coalfield, Edward Martin and of later writers wishing to perambulate the field after the old parochial manner, would start from Pontypool and proceed to the outskirts, first to Nantyglo and by Sirhowy to Dowlais, Merthyr and Hirwaun. Then on the wild district bordered by Banwaun, Graig-Y-Nos, Amman, Ty Llwyd to Gwendraeth and next Kidwelly. Here we would cross the sea to the Fidgety Pits and then to Landshipping Colliery and Saint Bride's Bay.

His tastes being more geological than archaeological, he would leave Saint David's unnoticed; turn around and cross the sea to Gower. Next leaving Swansea to the left, make his way to Tondu, Llantrisant, Caerphilly, Machen, Risca and end where he began at Pontypool.

This great coalfield is assumed by various authorities to be approximately 1,000 square miles, which are distributed as follows: Glamorganshire, 518 square miles; Monmouthshire, 104 square miles; Carmarthenshire, 228 square miles; Breconshire, 74 square miles and Pembrokeshire, 76 square miles.

Of the above, nearly 846 square miles are exposed, about 153 square miles lie beneath the sea and about one square mile is covered by newer formations.

The coalfield is one of rugged and mountainous character, the more hilly part characterised by a treeless expanse upon which the fern and heather, with scant herbage, form the most developed of its vegetation, while the margin ground of deeper soil, such as the old red sandstone affords, yields richer crops and loftier trees.

Nothing is more striking to the agriculturist than the contrast of soil afforded by the coal land, the limestone and the 'old red', all in close conjunction so to state. He finds the mineral land to be chilly and feeble in productive power, and to require all the appliances which agricultural chemistry suggests to improve that soil and to enable him to get anything like a moderate return for his labours; but the limestone is near at hand to assist and that which the mineral field lacks, he has on the one hand in the vale, prolific with its sea influences and on other the rich lands of Breconshire, to make ample amends.

Nature is parsimonious of her riches and refuses to give mineral wealth beneath and luxuriant crops above. Hence, in a similar way, the bleak districts of carboniferous limestone yield lead with only a thin soil above, the cold shales of Cardiganshire silver and the Snowdonian heights gold, with the scantiest covering of earth.

The coalfield is noticeable for its valleys, which all trend upon the Bristol Channel and are admirably adapted for railway and port.

The coal ground of highest elevation is Carn Moesan, on Craig y Llyn, a few miles from Hirwaun, where it has an elevation of 1,971ft above sea level. The lowest is on the Aberavon Burrows, where Messrs Vivian worked the Morfa pits beneath the low water mark of the Swansea Bay.

The thickness of the coal measures has been estimated by various authorities at from ten to twelve thousand feet.

Sir W.T. Lewis and Mr Morgan Reynolds, in a paper read before the South Wales Institute, stated that there was a greater thickness of coal in the Neath Valley than at any other part of the basin.

Now let us take one more glance at our field from another point of view. Its great cradle is the carboniferous limestone, resting upon its bed of old red sandstone. Between the carboniferous limestone, which is fossiliferous in a high degree, with its shell fish of pre-Adamite seas, are sandstones valuable in the making of steel, and the Farewell Rock, locally known as the Pudding Stone, from its containing quartz, the fragments of older rocks. We have said the cradle is the limestone. But instead of a cradle the bed might be more aptly described as in a stone box. It is a veritable stone box, where nature has stored her coals with limestone beneath and the Pennant slabs for the cover.

Now come and open it, and find the relics of an old world, which had its sunshine and its storms ages, vast beyond conception, before man came upon earth. Gathered here, carbonized where they fell, are the leaves and the branches and the trunks of the trees of old, with some few flowers and some bivalves that lived on pre-human shores and varying with the coal seams are measures of ironstone, sometimes so blended as to be worked together. The strong trunks of trees tell us of tropical growth and around them the most delicate tracery of stem and leaf, for so nature revelled in art and abundance when there was no audience of little, critical, sceptical man!

Three hundred years of patient investigation by the most gifted of our geologists, while fairly disclosing the extent of the coalfield, has not exhausted the catalogue of its flora and fauna. Nor has it ceased, let us add, now and then to disclose something from the workshop or laboratory of nature, by the side of which our relics of human genius, and skill and labour are but as the handiwork of yesterday. A finer scope for reflection could not be found than in looking upon the great store, with its remarkable arrangements, which have facilitated ease of working, thus showing that nature has acted in harmony with human intelligence, and by so doing yielded us a sermon in stone of the profoundest nature.

But we must pass on, and first show the photographic history of the South Wales Collieries beginning with the new important and influential stage of its development in the early 1800s of the South Wales Coalfield, the Cynon Valley.

Tower No.4 Colliery Hirwaun in 1991. Sinking began in 1941 and the pit opened in 1944.

The northern flank of the Rhigos Mountain at Hirwaun has been mined for over two centuries and the marks of early coal and iron working remain to this day.

Since the early 1800s various mines – both shafts and drifts – have operated under the name 'Tower'.

The mine centres on the No.3 Drift sunk in 1920, the 'Tower Sinkings' No.4 shaft 1941-44 and the No.3 New Drift 1958-59. In its early years, it belonged to the famous Crawshay family and later to Lord Merthyr. In 1935, it came under the ownership of the Powel-Duffryn Group, where it remained until nationalisation on 1 January 1947.

On 12 April 1962 at 10:30a.m. an explosion killed nine miners and another nine were injured, once again a reminder of the true price of coal.

In 1962, on the other side of the Rhigos, at the head of the Rhondda Fawr, Fernhill Collieries Nos 3 and 5 was planned for the link up with Tower and in 1964 Tower and Fernhill were 'linked' underground to form a single streamlined unit, employing 860 men and produced an annual tonnage of around 250,000. Its coal at this time was semi-anthracite, used for domestic heating and for the manufacture of the popular smokeless fuel 'Phurnacite'.

In 1978 the mining programme worked an area of around four square miles and took coal from the Five-Feet and the Nine-Feet seams at a maximum depth of 1,500ft below the surface. The 'take' was split by a series of geological faults, running roughly NW to SE, which threw down the line of the coal seams by varying distances, up to 164ft at their worst.

Within the mining operation, there were more than ten miles of underground roadways incorporating more than seven miles of high-speed belt conveyors. All the coal was taken by conveyor through to Tower, where it was washed and blended at the nearby coal preparation plant (washery).

At the Tower end particularly, the mine is bounded by extensive old iron workings dating back several hundred years and these need to be considered very carefully when planning new developments. There were substantial reserves in the Five-Feet and Nine-Feet seams.

In 1978 the average maximum demand of electrical power 3,293kW, the total capital value of plant and machinery in use £202,000 and the estimated workable coal reserves was 3.6m tons.

Tower Colliery Pit Bottom in 1996. The annual saleable output in 1978 was 244,021 tons, the average weekly output of saleable coal was 4,000 tons, the average output per man/shift at the coal face was 3.4 tons, the average output per man/shift overall was 1 ton, the deepest working level 1,500ft and the number of coal faces working were two. No.1 shaft, depth 518ft, diameter 16ft; No.2 shaft, depth 922ft, diameter 20ft; No.3 shaft depth, 880ft, diameter elliptical 17ft 6in by 11ft; manwinding capacity per cage wind 20; winding engines 300hp; drift length 3,000ft; coal conveying capacity per hour from pit 350tons; average weekly washery throughput 7,500 tons; types of coal semi-anthracite, markets domestic/manufactured smokeless fuels with a fan capacity of 200,000cu.ft per minute.

Tower No.4 Pit. Tower miners ready to descend the shaft in 1997. By April 1994 Tower was the last deep mine in the Cynon Valley and closure came on 23 April 1994. £2 million was raised by the 239 miners who pledged £8,000 each from their redundancy payments to achieve the buy-out and successfully the Tower Employees buy-out (TEBO) was won in October 1994 and on 23 December 1994 the ownership of Tower Colliery passed from British Coal to Goitre Tower Anthracite Ltd, the new name under which TEBO would operate. On 2 January 1995 Tower miners and their families and supporters marched back to the pit to take over its ownership and flew the Red Dragon of Wales on its headgear.

Now in the third millennium and six years on Tower's co-operative venture is producing anthracite coal from the V45 coalface in the Five-Feet coal seam. The development of the V47 coalface is also in progress. Week ending 25 March 2001 production. Face annual budget 590,551 tons, 39.93 cuts at 388 tons per cut (actual) 14,810 tons. Total (actual) saleable output to date 112,717 tons. Development advance V47 tail total 1,689yds, V47 faceline total 233yds. Total saleable output from development 954tons (approximate). Tower Colliery the last colliery in the Cynon Valley is still coaling today. November 2001.

Bryn-Y-Gwyddel, Llwydcoed licensed private coalmine in 1960. The mine was worked by John Davies and his brother in the 1950s.

Bwllfa Dare Colliery, Cwmdare No.1 and No.4 Pits in 1870. The 'Old Pit' Bwllfa No.1 upcast pit on the left in the photograph was opened in 1856 by E. Lewis and was sunk to a depth of 200yds to work the Gorllwyn, Nine-Feet, Bute, Yard and the Seven-Feet seams. The 'New Pit' Bwllfa No.4 pit downcast shaft on the right of the photograph was sunk to a depth of 150yds to work the Two-Feet-Nine, Four-Feet and the Six-Feet seams. Bwllfa Dare Colliery ceased coaling in 1936.

Bwllfa Dare No.1 Pit in 1870. The colliery was opened in 1856 by E. Lewis and worked by the Bwllfa Colliery Co. Ltd, J. Brogden & Sons, Bwllfa and Merthyr Dare Steam Coal Collieries (1881) Ltd until its closure in 1936. It was kept on a maintenance basis after closure until 1949 and came under a major reconstruction scheme that linked it to Mardy Colliery in the Rhondda Fach.

The Redevelopment of Bwllfa No.1 Pit on 13 July 1951. The manpower in 1913 was 1,333, in 1947 there was maintenance staff only, the manpower in 1955 was 282 with an output of 65,493tons and the manpower in 1956 was 188 with an output of 40,769tons.

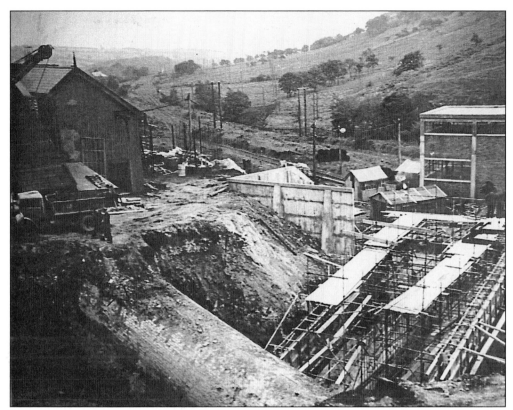

The Redevelopment of Bwllfa No.1 Pit. Laying the new fan drift in June 1952. The colliery fans were used to draw the stale air from the underground coal faces and roadways through the fan drift on the colliery surface and disperse it safely into the atmosphere.

Bwllfa No.1 Upcast Shaft in 1953 two years before the official opening of the newly developed colliery in 1955. At the proceedings were G.S. Morgan (production director, south western division), W. Whitehead (miners' agent NUM), J. John (vice chairman NACODS) and D. Thomas (organising secretary BACM).

Left: Maldwyn 'The hooker' James, manager of Mardy and Bwllfa Collieries in 1955. *Right:* Mr Tom Jones' invitation to the official opening of Bwllfa No.1 pithead baths on Saturday 8 January 1955. H. Watkins who had the longest unbroken service at Bwllfa Collieries in 1955 performed the opening ceremony.

Bwllfa No.1 Yellow Pit Bottom in 1956. Mardy Colliery pit bottom was 3,250yds from Bwllfa and a small journey of minecars (drams) were used to transport the miners from Bwllfa No.1 pit bottom to the coalfaces being worked at the Mardy Colliery underground districts.

Bwllfa No.1 Colliery. The 'Heavy Gang' in July 1989. Left to right: Gordon Williams (electrician), Norman Jones (pipe fitter), Malcolm 'Chick' Chambers (repairer), Steve Richards (fitter), Tony David (mechanical engineer), Gwyn Thomas (repairer), Bryn Bailey (electrician), John 'Gold watch and chain' Jones (fireman). Bwllfa No.1 Colliery was closed in 1989 by British Coal.

Nantmelyn Bwllfa No.2 Colliery Cwmdare in 1980. The colliery was sunk in 1860 by the Aberdare Merthyr Colliery Co. and was opened by Mordecai Jones of Morgannwg House, Brecon in 1866. Work quickly proceeded in the Four-Feet seam. It worked until 1895 when the company went into liquidation. Re-opened in 1898 by the Bwllfa Co. and in 1913 employed 973 with the Brickyard/Gorllwyn and New Drifts.

Nantmelyn Colliery in 1989. The remains of the underground stables at Nantmelyn, which was linked underground with Mardy colliery and was used for pumping mine water. In 1947 Nantmelyn employed 618 men and worked the Five-Feet, Six-Feet, Seven-Feet, Nine-Feet and the Gellideg seams. The 'Heavy Gang' dismantled the underground haulages and pumping station using a First Aid medical stretcher to recover the equipment.

Royston Jones colliery First Aid man and dismantler standing in the Nantmelyn underground pumping station on the last day of pumping on 5 July 1989. Roy is carrying a safety flame oil lamp for testing the presence of methane gas in the mine. Nantmelyn Colliery was closed in 1989 by British Coal.

18

Bwllfa No.3 Colliery, Cwmdare in the 1950s. Locally known as Powell's Pit was sunk in 1853 by Thomas Powell who worked it until 1872 and then it lay idle until 1905 when it was taken over by the Bwllfa Co. In 1913 Powell's Pit employed 342 men. The Bwllfa Co. worked the pit up to 1936. Powell's Pit closed in 1936.

Bwllfa No.4 Colliery, Cwmdare in 1920. The mine was opened in 1919 by the Bwllfa and Merthyr Dare Steam Coal Collieries (1881) Limited to the Nine-Feet seam and was locally known as the Four-Feet Drift. It was driven in to a length of 517yds. The drift was 11ft wide by 10ft high with a gradient of $7\frac{1}{2}$ in to 1yd and worked the Four-Feet seam. Bwllfa No.4 Colliery was a short life drift mine.

Windber Colliery Cwmdare in 1918. The mine opened in 1905. In 1913 employed seventy-three men and in 1920 employed 300 men producing 80,000 tons under the ownership of D.R. Llewellyn & Sons Ltd. Windber Colliery closed in the 1920s.

Cwmdu Uchaf Level Robertstown in 1920. The opening date and proprietor of this mine is unknown. In 1880 the Powell Duffryn Steam Collieries Ltd worked the level and in 1905 produced 7,559tons of large steam coal and 3,791tons of small steam coal. The mine was situated on the eastern side of the Cynon River. Cwmdu Uchaf Level was not in production in 1947.

Gadlys Colliery Gadlys in 1900. The colliery was sunk in 1802 and was locally known as the New Pit and the Victoria Pit. An explosion killed four miners at approximately 2.30a.m. on 4 October 1871. A horse was also killed and another one badly burnt at the head and neck and was so weak it had to be helped to its stall on the surface by two walls of men. Great tenderness was witnessed towards the poor horse. The colliery was owned by Waynes Merthyr Collieries when it closed in 1902.

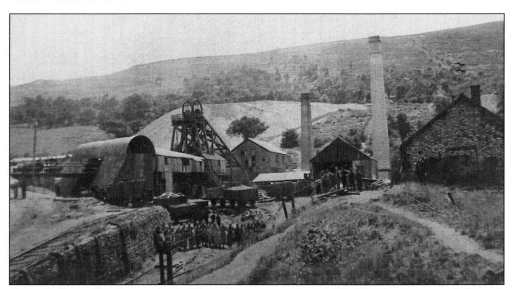

Graig Colliery Aberdare in 1901. The colliery was sunk in 1850. The downcast was 248 yards deep and the upcast shaft was known as the Gadlys Graig being a short distance from the Gadlys Colliery. In 1861 D.R. Llewellyn bought the colliery from the Aberdare Graig Coal Co. and produced 50,000tons of coal in 1920. Graig Colliery was acquired from Waynes Merthyr in 1947 by the National Coal Board.

Werfa Colliery Abernant in 1900. The Werfa Colliery was sunk in 1845 by John Nixon. The colliery worked the Bute, Nine-Feet, Six-Feet and the Red Vein seams. The wooden headgear was usually made from pitch pine for its strength and flexibly to withstand the weight of the sheaves, rope and the winding of men, coal, minerals and pit props etc. In May 1865 the proprietor was fined £5 for giving employment to eleven-year-old Charles Prothero who fell into the pit sump and drowned. Werfa Colliery closed in 1908.

Blaenant Colliery Abernant in 1900. Blaenant Colliery was sunk in the 1840s by the Aberdare Iron Co. On 31 October 1868 the accident reports show that twenty-eight-year-old collier Evan Evans was killed by a fall of roof. The colliery was worked by the Marquess of Bute and by the Powell Duffryn Steam Coal Co. and employed 500 men in 1913. Blaenant Colliery closed in 1927.

River Level Colliery Abernant in 1890. The River Level Colliery was worked in the 1870s by the Aberdare Plymouth Co. The photograph shows the colliery with a wooden headgear and the original winding ropes used at the colliery were flat. There is a reference of the colliery dating back to 1801. The photograph also shows the close proximity of the school and houses. A typical scene in the South Wales Coalfield. River Level Colliery ceased production in 1911.

De Winton Colliery Abernant in the 1880s. The De Winton Colliery was sunk in 1880 by James Lewis. The photograph shows one of the two shafts. The colliery was locally known as the Little Park and the Pwll Spite. It was situated just outside the perimeter fence of the drive in the grounds and gardens surrounding the Aberdare Hospital. De Winton Colliery closed in 1901.

Abernant No.9 Colliery Abernant in the early 1900s. The colliery was sunk in 1871 by the Abernant Iron Co. On 16 May 1890 the accident reports show that twenty-seven-year-old ripper W. Thomas and twenty-three-year-old haulier W. Rees were killed by an explosion of firedamp. The photograph includes the gaffers (bosses) and surface workers. The two women's work included greasing dram wheels, sheaves and surface hauliers.

Lletyshenkin Colliery Cwmbach in 1910 – it stood at 380ft OD (Ordnance Datum). The colliery was sunk in 1843 by William Thomas & Son and then it was owned by Burnyeat and Brown until 1872 when it was bought by the Powell Duffryn Steam Coal Co. On the 11 August 1849 an underground explosion killed fifty-two men and boys. In 1913 the Four-Feet and the Six-Feet seams were abandoned. Lletyshenkin Colliery closed in 1922.

Upper Duffryn Colliery Cwmbach in 1959. The colliery was sunk in 1843 to a depth of 94yds by David 'Alaw Goch' Williams. Seams mainly worked were the Nine-Feet and the Four-Feet. The colliery was also worked by the Powell Duffryn Steam Coal Co. Upper Duffryn Colliery closed in 1875.

Fforchaman Colliery Cwmaman in 1961. Locally known as Browns Pit the colliery was sunk in 1882 by David Williams and sold to Sir George Elliot of Powell Duffryn Steam Coal Co. in 1867. In 1954 the colliery worked the Five-Feet seam and with a manpower of 754 produced 158,000tons, in 1955 with a manpower of 732 produced 167,000tons, in 1956 with a manpower of 767 produced 174,000tons, in 1957 with a manpower of 765 produced 144,000tons, in 1958 with a manpower of 740 produced 137,000tons, in 1960 with a manpower of 653 produced 132,000tons and in 1961 with a manpower of 532 produced 127,000tons. Fforchaman Colliery was closed on 25 September 1965 by the National Coal Board.

Cwmaman Colliery Cwmaman in 1922. Two shafts were sunk by Thomas Shepherd in partnership with H.J. Evans and coal was struck in December 1849. The downcast shaft was sunk at a depth of 232yds to the Four-Feet seam and the upcast shaft was sunk to a depth of 218yds to the Two-Feet-Nine seam and in 1886 it was deepened to the Gellideg seam. From 1873 Thomas shepherd owned the colliery until the formation of the Cwmaman Coal Co. in 1882. The colliery merged with Fforchaman Colliery and in 1907 with a combined manpower of 1,800 produced 484,000tons, in 1911 with manpower of 2,050 produced 524,000tons and in 1919 with manpower of 1,921 produced 434,000tons. Cwmaman Colliery merged with Fforchaman Colliery and was closed on 25 September 1965 by the National Coal Board (NCB).

Fforchwen Colliery Cwmaman in 1919. Locally known as Bevans Pit, the sinking started in 1850 but was abandoned after 60yds. The shaft was finally completed in 1897 at a depth of 360yds and coal was produced in 1900. The colliery was worked by the Cwmaman Coal Co. Ltd and in 1913 employed 1,160 men. The colliery was absorbed into Cwmaman Colliery, which was closed in 1968 by the NCB.

Fforchwen Colliery Cwmaman in 1919. The photograph includes: W. Jones (colliery manager), R.R. Davies (agent), H.H. Merrett (director), D.R. Llewelyn (managing director), F.W. Mander (director) and two visitors. Lighthouse type battery operated safety lamps in use. The Concordia hand lamp weighed $9\frac{1}{2}$lb and the average weight of lamps used was 7lb.

Abergwawr Colliery Aberaman in 1880. Locally known as Plough Pit the colliery was sunk in 1854 by Thomas Powell. The colliery was owned by the Powell Duffryn Steam Coal Co. In 1872 the accident reports show that a ten-year-old boy was killed underground by a fall of roof. Abergwawr Colliery closed in 1886.

Aberaman Colliery Aberaman, Rescue Team in the 1920s. Aberaman rescue station closed in 1947. Aberaman Colliery stood at 437ft OD. It was opened in 1847 by Crawshay Bailey and was bought in 1866 by Sir George Elliot to form part of the new Powell Duffryn Steam Coal Co. In 1947 the colliery worked the Gellideg, Nine-Feet and the Five-Feet seams and in 1955 with a manpower of 591 produced 143,000tons, in 1956 with a manpower of 617 produced 137,000tons, in 1957 with a manpower of 662 produced 135,000tons, in 1958 with a manpower of 631 produced 137,000tons, in 1960 with a manpower of 578 produced 122,000tons and in 1961 with a manpower of 569 produced 114,000tons. Aberaman Colliery was closed on 23 November 1962 by the NCB.

Left: A Pay Docket belonging to fifteen-year-old trainee miner Garfield Evans, dated the 15 August 1959 with a take home pay of £5 10s 2d (£5.51). The Aberaman Colliery mining training centre served the South Western Division, No.4 area. *Right*: Aberaman Colliery in 1966. The colliery was retained as a training centre for the South Western Division, No.4 area. In 1923 the colliery employed 1,700 miners and 200 horses and was once the fastest coaling winding shaft in the world, raising 2,000tons in one shift.

Deep Duffryn Colliery Mountain Ash in 1967. The colliery was opened in 1850 by David Williams and George Insole and later developed by John Nixon to become part of the Nixons Navigation Coal Co. and was owned by the Powell Duffryn Steam Coal Co. prior to nationalisation on 1 January 1947. Deep Duffryn Colliery was closed in September 1979 by the NCB.

Deep Duffryn Colliery Underground Main Gate Road in 1970. The manpower in 1913 was 1,893. In 1947 the seams worked were the Yard and the Gellideg, in 1954, with a manpower of 646, the colliery produced 205,000tons, in 1955 with a manpower of 653, it produced 212,000tons, in 1956 with a manpower of 653, it produced 255,000tons, in 1957 with a manpower of 708, it produced 256,000tons, in 1958, with a manpower of 671, it produced 245,000tons, in 1960, with a manpower of 586, it produced 188,000tons and in 1961, with a manpower of 598, it produced 168,000tons.

Lower Duffryn Colliery Cwmpennar in 1910 – it stood at 498ft OD. Locally known as Cwmpennar being in the village of Cwmpennar was opened in the 1851 by Thomas Powell. The colliery was owned by the Powell Duffryn Steam Coal Co. prior to nationalisation in 1947. An underground explosion on the 25 February 1858 killed nineteen men and boys. Naked flame lights were in use. On the 6 November 1860 a further twelve miners were killed by an explosion and naked flame lights were also in use. Lower Duffryn Colliery ceased coaling in 1927 and was kept open for pumping mine water until the colliery was demolished in the 1970s.

Nixons Navigation Colliery Mountain Ash in 1900. Sinking of the colliery took place between 1863 and 1869. On 17 May 1890 the accident reports show that sixty-year-old collier G. Griffiths was killed by a fall of coal. Left of the pit headgear are wheels of a dram hoist. Nixons Navigation Colliery closed in 1940 and was used for emergencies as a second way out for Deep Duffryn Colliery.

Glyngwyn Level Miskin Mountain Ash in 1919. The mine opened in 1885 and worked the Rhondda No.3 seam and Rider. The miners in the photograph are standing timber known as the Collar and Arms using the Welsh Notch at the joints. Glyngwyn Level closed in 1925.

Cwmcynon Colliery, Penrhiwceiber, in 1940 – it stood at 786ft OD. The colliery was opened in 1895 by Nixons Navigation Coal Co. In 1913 the colliery employed 1,882 and in 1947 was acquired by the National Coal Board. The seams worked were the Six-Feet, Nine-Feet and the Four-Feet seams, and employed 489 men. Cwmcynon Colliery was closed in 1949 by the NCB.

Penrikyber Colliery Penrhiwceiber in 1907. The colliery was started in 1872 by Mr David Thomas of Cwmbach, on behalf of a group of businessmen who formed the Penrikyber Navigation Collieries Co. Despite the many problems caused by frequent encounters with soft sand beds and running water, the first commercial coal was coming out of the pit by 1879 and was raise by a crude wooden headgear with a single rope. By 1901 steel headgear had replaced this early structure and the No.2 shaft had been fitted with a powerful steam winder, which operated continuously until its electrification in 1957. A third shaft was added to the mine in 1912, but coal winding ceased in 1949 and the shaft was maintained for pumping mine water only.

The original owners soon came under the control of Cory Brothers and in the peak years of the 1920s the colliery employed nearly 2,000 men. For most of this period and well into the 1930s Penrikyber produced an average 350,000tons of good steam coal each year.

In 1943 a company takeover brought Penrikyber into the Powell Duffryn Steam Coal Co. where it remained until nationalisation.

A £1 million reorganisation in the early 1960s streamlined loading and conveying underground and in 1978 the 800 man pit produced around an annual 180,000 tons for the Phurnacite and domestic fuel markets.

The mining programme at this time worked an area of around four square miles, bounded by two major geological faults, the Werfa on the east and the Gadlys/Ynysybwl, dividing it from neighbouring Lady Windsor Colliery on the west. Coaling was in the Seven-Feet and the Gellideg seams and the coalfaces under the mountain to the west were operating at a depth from the surface of 2,400ft. There were more than ten miles of underground roadways involved in the operation and over three miles of high-speed belt conveyors in daily use.

Variations in the burning qualities of Penrikyber coals in 1978 meant that various different customer needs a useful marketing flexibility!

The Two-Feet-Nine coal seam was at a depth of 1,521ft, the Four-Feet 1,581ft, the Six-Feet 1,638ft, the Nine-Feet 1,749ft, the Yard 1,863ft, the Seven-Feet 1,893ft and the Five-Feet/Gellideg 1,968ft.

Penrikyber Colliery No.1 Pit Bottom in 1978. With a manpower of 804 the colliery produced around an annual saleable output of 176,324tons; with an average weekly saleable output of 4,000tons; an average output per man/shift at the coal face 4.4tons; the average output overall per man/shift was 1.2tons; the deepest working level 2,400ft; the number of coal faces working in 1978 were three. Shaft No.1: depth 1,758ft, diameter 16ft 6in; shaft No.2: depth 1,955ft, diameter 16ft 6in; man winding capacity per cage wind 48; coal winding capacity per cage wind 5tons; winding engines horsepower 2,000/2,030; average weekly washery throughput 5,700tons; types of coal: prime steam. Markets: smokeless fuels/power stations; Fan capacity: 180,000cu. ft per minute; Average maximum demand of electrical power: 3,900kW; total capital value of plant and machinery in use in 1978 was £567,597 and the estimated workable coal reserves was estimated at 4.6m tons. Penrikyber Colliery was closed in 1985 by the NCB.

Carne Park Level Abercynon in 1904. The mine was opened in 1864 by Park Newydd Colliery Co. The colliers are wearing cloth caps and using naked flame lights. The fireman (colliery official) is using a safety oil lamp to test the presence of gas (firedamp). The Daren No.2 coal seam was worked. Carne Park Level closed in 1965.

Nantyfedw Level Abercynon in 1967. The mine opened in 1916. The last owners were the Blacker Bros of Penrhiwceiber. The Daren No.2 coal seam was worked which was also known as the stinking vein because of the high sulphur content given out when the coal was being burnt. The miner in the dram is haulier Harry Rogers. The horse Suzy wearing a battery operated cap lamp was treated like a family pet by the workmen and the miners would take apples, fresh carrots and sugar to work every day for their working friends. During the First World War hundreds of horses were taken from the pits to the front in France and they were affectionately missed. Horses working underground in wet and dusty conditions suffered with many illnesses including pneumoconiosis. In 1914 there were 17,000 horses employed in the South Wales Coalfield, by 1974 there were just 150 horses employed and the last horses in the Coalfield retired on 25 May 1999 – to begin a life in genteel retirement, paid for with a 'pension' fund that many of us would envy. Gremlin and Robbie, who have spent their lives pulling drams at Pantygasseg a private mine in South Wales, were the last beneficiaries of a charitable fund worth £500,000. They pulled one-ton drams from the coalface 500yds inside the mine and worked from 8.00a.m. to 4.00p.m. five days a week – the same hours as the men. At weekends they rested in a nearby meadow. Nantyfedw Colliery was closed in 1972 by the NCB.

Coalmining Historian Harry Rogers of Abercynon with his mining artefacts in 2001. Also a retired miner, Harry Rogers has a superb private collection of mining history, including: coalmining surface and underground plans of coal seams, coalface and districts; explosion reports; naked flame and battery safety lights; tools and small mining equipment; surveying instruments; photographs; documents and accurate detailed models of pits, levels and coalfaces which he has hand made. Harry Rogers has a mine of information on the history of the South Wales Coalfield; he has been a good friend and I sincerely thank him for all his help over the years.

Abercynon Colliery, Abercynon, in 1988, at the junction of the Taff and Cynon Valleys. The Dowlais Iron Co. sank, between 1889 and 1896, the shafts of their Dowlais Cardiff Colliery. It was the last sinking in the Cynon Valley and finally closed in 1986. By the turn of the century, the pit had passed into the ownership of Guest, Keen & Nettlefold and in the peak years of the 1920s employed over 2,500 men. In 1930, Welsh Associated Collieries took control, but were themselves later absorbed into the Powell Duffryn Steam Coal Co., then known as Abercynon Colliery, they remained its owners until nationalisation in 1947. The collieries bright blue headgear became something of a landmark to travellers on the A470 trunk road between Cardiff and Merthyr Tydfil. Following the publication in 1973 of 'Plan For Coal' a massive capital investment programme was launched by the NCB, aimed at securing the nation's vital energy supplies well into the next century.

For South Wales alone, over £100 million was earmarked for major modernisation projects to streamline long-life pits, to locate and log new coal reserve, to create new mines and to link established neighbouring pits into single, high-production units – Britain's guarantees in a fuel-hungry future!

Abercynon shaft No.1: depth, 2,217ft; diameter, 20ft; shaft No.2: depth, 2,260ft; diameter, 20ft; man winding capacity per cage wind, 48; coal winding capacity per cage wind, 6tons; winding engine horsepower, 1,600.

In 1974 parallel tunnels one 1,000 yards and the other almost a mile were driven beneath the mountain separating Lady Windsor Colliery from Abercynon Colliery. This was the start of a £500,000 project designed to link the two collieries, forming a single streamlined unit, bringing all the coal out from the Lady Windsor end, for blending and washing, ready for its eventual markets. High speed belt conveyors, under remote control from Lady Windsor, sped the coal into a 400tons spiral bunker shaft, fitted with 'nucleonic' capacity monitoring, the first of its kind in any British Coalfield, as part of a new £3m scheme to exploit the reserves to the west of Lady Windsor shafts.

Abercynon Colliery Mines Rescue Team in 1910. Abercynon rescue station closed in 1929. Abercynon/Lady Windsor Collieries. Sinking began at Lady Windsor colliery in 1884 and the pit opened in 1885. The combined unit worked an area of around six square miles, bounded on the east by the Werfa fault and on the west by the Tŷ Mawr fault. Geological conditions within the 'take' were amongst the worst in South Wales. Despite this, the pit managed to extract an annual 250,000tons of prime coking coal, from the Nine-Feet, Seven-Feet, Bute and the Five-Feet/Gellideg seams. Joe Gormley, the president of the Mineworkers Union, described Lady Windsor/Abercynon as 'a dammed good pit under very difficult conditions'.

The pit had what the manager described as 'a wall full of safety awards'. In the NCB national safety competition in 1977, it was placed top in South Wales. Manpower, 1,190. In 1978 the colliery produced an annual saleable output of 248,430tons; an average weekly saleable output of 7,500tons; an average output per man/shift at the coal face 1.1tons; the deepest working level 2,100ft; the number of coal faces working in 1978 was five; the Lady Windsor shaft No.1: depth, 2,057ft; diameter, 19ft; shaft No.2: depth, 2,060ft; diameter, 17ft; man winding capacity per cage wind, 18; coal winding capacity per cage wind, 3tons; winding engines, 1,250hp; average weekly washery throughput, 11,000tons; types of coal coking, markets coke and industrial/domestic smokeless fuels; fan capacity 240,00cu.ft per minute; average maximum demand of electrical power, 3,972kW; total capital value of plant and machinery in use in 1978, £3.05m; and the estimated workable coal reserves were 19.6m tons.

The Two-Feet-Nine seam was at a depth of 1,587ft, the Four-Feet, 1,630ft; the Six-Feet, 1,684ft; the Nine-Feet, 1,803ft; the Yard seam, 1,870ft; the Seven-Feet, 1,890ft and the Five-Feet/Gellideg, 1,950ft.

To win these precious coal seams good winding equipment was the key to any deep mine as it responsible for conveying men and every single item of material and machinery into and out of the pit. The winding house was generally the largest of the surface buildings at a colliery, accommodating the huge engines and winding drums. By erecting one large engine house to take all the main machinery, the necessary room could be obtained at less capital cost than by constructing separate buildings and was also more convenient and efficient to operate.

Lady Windsor Colliery, Ynysybwl, in 1914 – height 491ft OD. Sinking began at Lady Windsor colliery in 1884 and the pit opened in 1885. On 8 May 1896 the accident reports show that twenty-three-year-old haulier J. Hughes was found dead under a loaded dram, having apparently fallen off the gun.

Lady Windsor Colliery Pit Bottom in 1979. On 15 September 1898 the accident reports show that fifty-five-year-old hitcher W. Jones was killed while scotching a loaded dram on the cage, another one ran forward to the shaft and crushed him between the two drams. The Lady Windsor Colliery and Abercynon Colliery were closed in 1986 by the NCB.

Albion Colliery, Cilfynydd, in 1894. The Albion Colliery, in the Taff Valley, was situated in close proximity to Abercynon Colliery and was sunk between 1884 and 1887 when the two shafts reached a depth of 1,900ft. It was opened by the Albion Steam Coal Co. who went into liquidation in 1928. The colliery was bought by the Powell Duffryn Steam Coal Co.

On Saturday 23 June 1894 an explosion killed 290 men and boys in the No.1 district called Grovers Level. The No.1 district had forty-one working places.

The explosion occurred in the Four-Feet seam, which was at a depth of 545yds from the surface, the thickness of the seam varied from between 5ft 10in and 6ft 10in. Grovers level had reached 1,136yds from the shafts on the western side of the pit.

Apart from the deaths of six men in two separate accidents when the pit was sunk, Albion Colliery, Cilfynydd, was to remain untouched by the spectre of death for the first few years of its life. At 3:50p.m. on 23 June 1894, nearly two hours after the afternoon shift had descended to repair the roadways and remove dust, two loud reports were heard above ground in quick succession. These were followed immediately by a charge of dust and smoke from the downcast shaft and then from the upcast shaft. Men on the surface near the shafts were blown backwards by the blasts and temporarily blinded by the dust. No flame was reported, but it was quite probable that some flame reached the top of the downcast shaft for those there declared they had felt the heat of the blast and two of them complained that their eyelashes had been singed.

The muffled roar of an explosion, followed by a tremor shook the whole valley, and brought inhabitants of the village hurrying to their doors. Like so many of the narrow mining valleys of South Wales, the small terraced cottages perched precariously on the steep hillsides overlooking the pit. From such a vantage point, those who looked onto the valley below saw dense swirling clouds of smoke shrouding the shafts. The whole community held its breath and feared the worst. The news soon began to reach those outside the community, and crowds began to arrive in there hundreds from the Cynon Valley, Pontypridd and Rhondda Valley and the Merthyr Valleys.

Messages of sympathy flowed into the stunned community, one was sent on behalf of Queen Victoria.

By 6 July the total loss of human life was put at 279, although twenty-five men were still unaccounted for. The situation was not helped by the fact that several of the victims had been buried without being identified. As work on clearing the mine progressed, two more victims were located and brought to the surface. These, together with the death of one of the remaining survivors, brought the official figure of those who perished in the disaster to 290. The horses that had been in the deep were found alive.

The Coroner's findings were recorded thus: The cause of the explosion was unknown, but it was believed to have occurred by the ignition of coal dust following an explosion of firedamp.

Albion Colliery in 1900. The colliery was reopened within two weeks following the explosion on 23 June 1894 and some changes in safety took place. The old spray system had not proved successful and was replaced by hosepipes and the coal drams had been altered to prevent coal falling on the roadways and being crushed into fine dust. The safety Clanny lamp that was used had a single gauze and an automatic lock that could be opened only by a powerful electro-magnet. The lamps were lit by an electric spark by an apparatus consisting of a square iron box with a locked door. On top of the box was a dish on which was placed the lamp to be relit. In the box was a double accumulator connected to an induction coil, the accumulator being charged with 4V. The current could be increased to the coil by up to 10,000V. If a lamp was not placed correctly on the dish on top of the box the spark produced to light it would fail to pass through an insulated pin and ignite the wick, but would instead make contact between the lamp housing and the coil. If gas was present then there could be disastrous results.

Approximately 3:10p.m. on the 10 November 1906 an explosion killed the following six men while working the No.1 seam: Thomas Prosser, master haulier, aged forty-one; Richard Hughes, timberman, aged thirty-three; Abraham Lloyd, assistant timberman, aged twenty-one; Francis Strong, assistant timberman, aged forty; John Jones, ripper, aged thirty-six; and James Henry Hill, overman, aged fifty-three.

The overman James Henry Hill was sent underground to investigate and found a large fall in the main roadway, but was able to by-pass it by going through another heading. He came to the lamp station and found five very badly burned workmen. Three were dead and the other two died in their homes within forty-eight hours. Henry Hill continued to search, but went missing and a rescue party found his body later. He had died from the effects of after-damp.

On the 26 November the following verdict was recorded by the jury:

In view of the theory advanced by Mr Lewis, the agent of the colliery, supported by HM Inspectors, that the explosion was probably caused by the emission of sparks from the electric battery, we are agreed upon that theory and that no fault or negligence can be attached to any persons concerned.

It appears that the relighter had been put in what the manager considered was a safe place in the intake nine months prior to the accident. The box was kept locked so as not to be available for use except by the person authorised by the manager to relight lamps. It had, however, been removed from its brick built casing at 2:00p.m. on the day of the explosion for fear of a fall of roof which would occur when timbers were removed as part of the repair programme. According to the manager, even if the relighter had not been removed from its original position the man in charge would have taken the extinguished lamps to it and the same result would have ensued. Everyone agreed with this, but between the accident and the resumed inquest the manager reported that all relighters in the colliery had been removed and resited near the downcast shaft. The Albion colliery was closed in September 1966 by the NCB.

Tower Colliery is the last remaining deep mine in the Cynon Valley, 2001.

In everlasting memory to the miners who lost their lives in the Cynon Valley from 1845 to 1853

Date	Mine	Lives Lost
1 Aug 1845	Old Duffryn and Lletyshenkin	27 killed and 1 injured
2 Aug 1845	Cwmbach	28 killed
16 May 1849	Werfa	3 killed and 2 injured
11 Aug 1849	Lletyshenkin	52 killed
14 Dec 1850	New Duffryn	13 killed
10 May 1852	Duffryn	20 killed
12 Aug 1852	Dowlais Level	Collier William Phillips (40) killed by falling top coal.
21 Sept 1852	Duffryn Dare	Sinker William Lewis (20) killed by blast explosion when boring out the charge
8 Oct 1852	Cwmbach	Colliers David Llewellyn (26) and William Griffith (27) killed by explosion of firedamp.
19 Oct 1852	Aberaman	Collier John Morgan (60) killed by clod falling in Upper Four-Feet seam
1 Nov 1852	Gadlys	Doorboy Benjamin Robert (13) killed by fall of coal from pillar.
16 Dec 1852	Middle Duffryn	David Jenkins (32) killed by a fall of coal.
6 Jan 1853	Gadlys	Collier Samuel Franklin (49) killed by falling down the pit.
18 Jan 1853	Werfa Sinker	Thomas Owen (55) killed by a fall of stone which broke the staging in staple shaft.
23 Jan 1853	Abernant-Y-Groes	Engineman William Ellis (26) killed by falling down the pit whilst intoxicated.
12 Feb 1853	Blaengwawr	Collier Rees Meredith (31) killed by explosion of firedamp from neglect of a door.
16 Feb 1853	Cwrthouse	Collier William Havard (23) killed by fall of coal in first stall.
23 Feb 1853	Lletyshenkin	Doorkeeper John Johns (10) killed by falling under dram.
2 May 1853	Upper Duffryn	Colliers David Howells (30) and Morgan Nicholas (30) by the rope breaking on hanging staging.
9 May 1853	New Pit	Sinker Jos Trewarthar (43) killed when side of shaft fell on hanging staging.
25 July 1853	Cwmaman	Haulier Morgan Williams (21) killed by coal falling off a dram.
4 Aug 1853	Werfa	Labourer John Smith (40) killed when a coal dram was tipped on him.
31 Aug 1853	Werfa	Collier John Davies killed when struck by drams.
9 Sep 1853	Abernant	Colliery John Williams (21) killed by a fall of roof.
12 Sep 1853	Cwmbach	Doorboy John Evans (11) killed by an explosion of firedamp.
15 Sep 1853	Lletyshenkin	Doorboys John Williams (12) and David Thomas (11) and collier William Rees (65) were killed by an explosion of firedamp from using naked light in pillar workings. Fifteen others were injured. The manager John Johns was found incompetent; rules and repeated cautions had been systematically violated. Verdict of manslaughter was found at the coroner's inquest against owner David Simms.
16 Sep 1853	Gadlys	Fireman Rees Williams (37) was killed by a fall of roof.
26 Sep 1853	Cefn Pennar	Labourer Oliver Jones (12) fell off carriage whilst riding down a surface incline and was killed.
3 Oct 1853	River Level	Collier Lewis Griffiths (52) was killed by a fall of roof.
17 Oct 1853	Lletyshenkin	Collier John Davies (23) fell off staging while descending the pit and was killed. The guides were found to be unsafe.
2 Nov 1853	Gadlys	Collier John Williams (47) was killed by a fall of roof.
8 Nov 1853	Aberaman	Collier David Jones (24) was killed by a fall of coal.
18 Nov 1853	Aberaman	Collier John Davies (40) was killed by a fall of coal.
29 Nov 1853	Cwm Neol	Miner William Lewis (22) was knocked of staging in pit by water splashing and killed.
29 Nov 1853	Gadlys	Collier Richard Morgan (23) was killed by a fall of coal.

Once again a sad reminder of the true price of coal. A sudden change; at God's command they fell; They had no chance to bid their friends farewell, Swift came the blast, without a warning given, And bid them haste to meet their God in Heaven.

Two

The Rhondda Valley in the South Wales Coafield

Back in the early years of the nineteenth century the Rhondda Valleys were pleasant deep-set wooded vales and were even more beautiful than that of the Taff, being more wild and grand, and bearing a general resemblance to the Wye. The charming picturesque valleys had rivulets so clear that the term 'Rhondda' is derived, according to some authorities, from two words meaning 'good water'. The syllable *Rhon* is associated with the names 'Rhone' and 'Rhine', two of the major rivers of Europe, and *da* (in its mutated form 'dda') is the Welsh word for good. The 'good water' of the Rhonda Valley streams had, however, been blackened for more than 100 years by the coal from the pits that were sunk, one every mile or so, along the base of the valleys. Around these pits grew the villages for the mineworkers, becoming townships, which eventually linked up their terraces in almost continuous succession along the valleys to provide housing for a population, which at its maximum was 167,000.

When people talk about the South Wales Coalfield they almost invariably think of 'The Rhondda Valley', the most intensively mined area in the world. The Welsh usage 'Cwm Rhondda', meaning Rhondda Valley, is somewhat misleading because there are two valleys, the 'Big Rhondda', 'Y Rhondda Fawr', and the 'Little Rhondda', 'Y Rhondda Fach'. The Rhondda Fawr is fourteen miles long, extending from Pontypridd, where it joins the Vale of Taff, to Blaenrhondda at the northern end. The Rhondda Fach is seven miles long, from Porth (at the junction with the Rhondda Fawr) to Maerdy at the northern end.

Looking back over the years it can today be seen that the history of coal mining in the Rhondda Valleys follows the pattern of that of the coalfield the intense and unregulated development from 1870 to 1913 then in February 1917, Britain's coal industry was completely reorganised and brought under government control. The Board of Trade regulated the output and distribution of coal, the recruitment of miners was curtailed and price control was introduced. During this period of state control, wages, labour conditions and hours of work, too, were regulated on a national basis. But there was no control of profits and Rhondda Coalowners continued to enjoy exceptionally high profits during the period of state control. Grossly exaggerated accounts continued to appear describing the high wages earned by the Rhondda colliers during the war years. Doubtless these years were generally a period of economic prosperity for the miners and their families, but the prosperity was of short duration and was by no means as much as is usually supposed. Miners wages rose throughout the period of the First World War, but this was accompanied by a steep rise in the price of all commodities, so that, for most of the period, wages continually lagged behind the rise in prices. There were years of increasing difficulty between 1914 and 1946, except for a brief period in the early 1920s, then came the reorganisation and planned redevelopment initiated by the NCB when the mines came under public ownership on 1 January 1947.

The Rhondda communities owe their existence to the coal-mining industry though today the dependence on that industry has completely gone.

In the late 1950s and early 1960s nearly 13,000 men worked at thirteen collieries and produced approximately 2,900,000tons of coal a year, or nearly one-seventh of the output of the South Wales Coalfield. This meant that 46,000 people, nearly half the population of the

Rhondda, had a direct family association with the coal-mining industry. Many of the people of the Rhondda now work in factories etc. outside the Rhondda, or are engaged on the various activities of a busy community. All the factories depended on coal to supply them with fuel and power, either as coal in its prime form, or as coke, or as electricity and gas obtained from coal, the people who ran the shops, the buses, the churches, the schools, the railways, the public house, the cinemas and so on, all had a vital concern with the successful operation of the coal-mining industry both in respect of its product and in the economic wellbeing of the town for the wages paid for winning that product. It was said that if coal stops coming up from the Rhondda Pits the life of the community will also come to a halt!

In less than a generation such singular beauty of the South Wales valleys had been lost forever. The river Rhondda became a dark, turgid, and contaminated gutter, into which is poured the refuse of the host collieries, which skirt the fourteen miles of its course. The hills had been stripped of all their woodland beauty, and they stood rugged and bare, with immense rubbish heaps covering their surface. The whole valley had become transformed, the din of steam engines, the whirr of machinery, the grating sound of coal screen, and the hammering of the smithies proceed increasingly night and day, year in year out An unheard of wealth of industry and a great populace have simultaneously sprung up together during the coal rush. The industrial townships of the valley appeared to be inseparably connected in one continuous series of streets of workmen's cottages from Pontypridd through the Rhondda Valley, the Ely Valley and the Cynon Valley, from where hung a perpetual smoke cloud from the vast furnaces which were always busy smelting iron and steel from the neighbouring coalfields. An unremitting and wholesale plunder in the name of industrial progress brought about such a stark transformation, witnessed on a similar scale throughout the breadth of the valleys. So extensive did the exploitation become that eventually almost 200 collieries had raised coal from the valleys. Statistics showed the distribution of working pits: seventy-five in the Cynon Valley, sixty-six in the Rhondda Valley, fifty-six in the Taff-Ely Valleys.

The pioneering ventures were at the lower end of the Rhondda Fawr valley in the district around Dinas. A Dr Richard Griffiths opened levels in the 1790s and Walter Coffin followed his efforts on a bigger scale in the early years of the nineteenth century. By the 1840s Coffin's Colliery at Dinas was producing 1,000tons a week. With the extension of the Taff Vale Railway other prospectors began operations near the junction of the two valleys. But compared with the developments at a later stage they were still scratching the surface. The deeper seams were not located and the possibilities in the middle and upper districts of the Rhondda valleys were viewed with scepticism.

It was the Taff Vale Railway Co. who stimulated enterprise by offering an award of £500 to the first prospector to sink a pit and strike a seam of coal in the Upper Rhondda.

Name of Seam	Depth (Yards)			
	Great Western	Lewis Merthyr	Clydach Vale	Mardy No.1 Pit
Rhondda No.2	79	41		
Rhondda No.3	148	115	61	
Pentre		228	217	185
Gorllwyn		250		195
Two-Feet-Nine	344	330	340	273
Four-Feet	364	354	359	284
Six-Feet	387	377	402	291
Red Vein	405	392	430	300
Nine-Feet	417	399	453	320
Five-Feet	470	429		366
Gellideg	503	453	526	378

Penrhiw Colliery, Gyfeillion, in 1897. The colliery was sunk by the Great Western Colliery Co. to the Rhondda No.2 seam in 1880. In 1900 the colliery employed 200 men and ceased production in 1922. The colliery was owned by the Powell Duffryn Steam Coal Co. prior to nationalisation in 1947 and kept open for pumping mine water from Cwm Colliery. The colliery wooden headgear was the last in the South Wales Coalfield and was dismantled in 1964.

Maritime Colliery, Pontypridd, in the early 1900s. The colliery was also known as the Pontypridd Colliery and was sunk in 1841 by John Edmunds to the Rhondda No.3 seam at a depth of 60yds and was worked by the water balance method. In 1906 the shaft was deepened to 390yds. In 1954 with a manpower of 404 the colliery produced an annual saleable output of 96,000tons, in 1955 with a manpower of 338 produced 78,167tons, in 1956 with a manpower of 398 produced 74,787tons, in 1957 with a manpower of 413 produced 85,738tons and in 1960 with a manpower of 357 produced 82,842tons. The colliery was owned by the Powell Duffryn Steam Coal Co. prior to nationalisation in 1947. Maritime Colliery was closed in June 1961 by the NCB.

Newbridge Colliery, Pontypridd, in 1894. The colliery was sunk in 1844 by John Calvert to the Rhondda No.3 seam at a depth of 54yds. The colliery was the first in the area to use a steam engine for winding and was worked by the Newbridge and Rhondda Coal Co. until the 1880s and then by the Crawshay Bros until its closure. On 12 March 1874 the accident reports show that forty-five-year-old fireman (colliery official) T. Jones was killed by a fall of stone. Newbridge Colliery closed in 1897.

Pwllgwaun Colliery, Pwllgwaun, in 1900. The colliery was opened by Daniel Thomas in 1875 to the Rhondda No.2 seam and was locally known as Dan's Muck Hole. In 1913 the colliery employed twenty-eight miners; in 1937, with a manpower of fifty-two, the colliery produced an annual saleable output of 12,000tons of coal. In 1947 only twenty-five men were employed. Pwllgwaun Colliery was closed in 1948 by the NCB.

Tŷ Mawr Colliery, Hopkinstown, in 1900. The colliery was sunk in 1923 by the Great Western Colliery Co. The average seam sections were: Two-Feet-Nine, 58in at a depth of 349yds; Four-Feet, 77in at a depth of 365yds; Six-Feet, 81in at a depth of 392yds; Red-Coal, 40in at a depth of 409yds; Nine-Feet, 68in at a depth of 421yds; Lower-Four-Feet, 76in at a depth of 442yds; and the Five-Feet at 68in at a depth of 475yds. In 1954 with a manpower of 860 the colliery produced an annual output of 250,000tons; in 1955 with a manpower of 850 it produced 230,517tons; in 1956 with a manpower of 873 it produced 221,882tons; in 1957 with a manpower of 900 it produced 240,297tons; and in 1958 with a manpower of 852 it produced 339,595tons.

Tŷ Mawr NUM Lodge Banner. The colliery was owned by the Powell Duffryn Steam Coal Co. prior to nationalisation in 1947. The last dram of coal was raised on 21 June 1983. Tŷ Mawr Colliery was merged with Lewis Merthyr Colliery in 1958 and was closed in 1983 by the NCB.

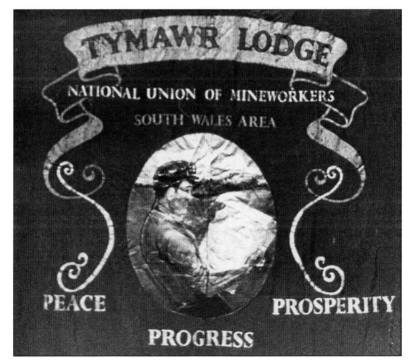

The Great Western Colliery, Hopkinstown, in 1901. The height of the colliery was 293ft OD and it was sunk in 1848 by John Calvert to the Rhondda No.3 seam at a depth of 149yds. The colliery was leased to the Great Western Railway Co. for ten years in 1854 and sold to the Great Western Colliery Co. in 1866. Three more shafts were sunk in the 1870s. On 12 August 1892 an explosion killed sixty-three (from the actual report) men and boys.

The Great Western Colliery Officials in 1929. Back row, second left, is John Martin Thomas. On 4 December 1874 the accident reports show that thirty-five-year-old stoker H. Marslyn was killed by falling down the pit while engaged in disconnecting drums. On 11 April 1893 an explosion killed sixty men and boys. The three winding shafts were used by the mines rescue team and the rescuers. The Great Western Colliery closed in 1923.

The Great Western Colliery AFC Cup Winners in the 1929/30 season. On 5 July 1875 the accident reports show that thirty-four-year-old fireman (colliery official) J. Prosser was killed by a fall of stone. On 1 January 1884 the accident reports also show that twenty-two-year-old mason Griffiths Davies and twenty-three-year-old mason Alfred Cornish were killed by a fall of stone.

The Hetty Colliery Winding Engine House, Hopkinstown, on 16 April 2000. The Hetty shaft was sunk by the Great Western Colliery Co. in 1875 to the Six-Feet seam at a depth of 392yds. Barker & Cope of Kidsgrove, Staffordshire, built the steam-winding engine in 1875 and was originally built with two 40in cylinders with Cornish valves, it was later fitted with new 36in cylinders and piston valves. The drum has a diameter of 16ft and originally held a flat rope. Brian Davies curator of the Pontypridd Historical Centre has restored the winding engine, which is now in working order and will be open to the public in the near future.

Lewis Merthyr Colliery, Trehafod, in 1954. The height of the colliery was 303ft 6in OD, National Grid ref. 03969113. Sunk to 1,418ft 10in. The site of Lewis Merthyr Colliery had been worked from as long ago as 1850, when brothers David and John Thomas leased the mineral rights of Hafod Fach and Nyth Bran Farm and opened the Hafod Colliery in 1850. In the 1870s W.T. Lewis, later Lord Merthyr, bought the Coed Cae and Hafod Collieries and called the new concern Lewis Merthyr Colliery. He then commenced to sink the Bertie shaft and by 1890 the Trefor shaft which completed the Lewis Merthyr Colliery. In 1881 the Lewis Merthyr Navigation Collieries Ltd was formed and by 1891 it was changed to Lewis Merthyr Consolidated Collieries Ltd. The colliery was owned by the Powell Duffryn Steam Coal Co. prior to nationalisation in 1947.

The Bertie shaft was 14ft 1in diameter and 1.418ft 10in depth. The Winding Engine was unique because of the unusual design of drum known as a differential bi-cylindro conical drum, which enabled the engine to wind to and fro and from different depths simultaneously. There is though to have existed only one other engine of this style. The engine was originally steam operated until it was electrified in the late 1950s.

In 1958, the NCB invested £1.2m in a surface and underground reorganisation, to merge and streamline the two mines. Lewis Merthyr and Tŷ Mawr employed 730 men and produced an average annual output of around 132,000tons.

The working area was almost twelve square miles and incorporated around twenty-one miles of underground roadways, in which there were over $3\frac{1}{2}$ miles of high-speed belt conveyors in daily use.

Lewis Merthyr Colliery in 1905. The colliers in the photograph are boring a hole with a bow (hand drill) in the coal seam in preparation for shot-firing. On 22 November 1956 an explosion killed two men outright with another seven dying later. The pit ceased winding coal in 1958 on its merger with Tŷ Mawr Colliery. Lewis Merthyr Colliery and Tŷ Mawr Colliery were both closed in 1983 by the NCB.

Visitors on an underground tour at the Lewis Merthyr Colliery, now the Rhondda Heritage Park on 3 October 1998. In 1913 the manpower in the Bertie Pit was 1,095, in 1947 the manpower was 1,107 and in the Trefor Pit 986. In 1954 with a combined manpower of 1,186 it produced 281,986tons and in 1955 with a manpower of 1,506 it produced 249,211tons.

The Rhondda Heritage Park. On 13 May 2000 actor Glyn Houston, on the left in the photograph, unveiled a memorial to the thousands of miners who died in the South Wales Collieries. The memorial is in the form of a 6ft-high miners lamp, complete with an eternal flame, which will stand as a lasting tribute to all the miners who died while working in the pits. In the early years of the establishment of the Heritage Park, substantial work had to be done. This involved extensive landscaping including making six shafts safe and generally transforming the site from one of dereliction and decay, to a first-class amenity.

Left: The Hafod Colliery in 1920. David and John Thomas leased the mineral rights of Hafod Fach and Nyth Bran Farm and opened the Hafod Colliery in 1850. The Coed Cae No.1 and No.2 was sunk in 1850, the Bertie in 1880 and the Trefor in 1890. From 1870, all the Lewis Merthyr Colliery operations belonged to William Thomas Lewis, later Lord Merthyr. Lewis Merthyr Colliery was formed from six shafts into the same workings. In 1913 the manpower in the Hafod was 1,130. In 1929 they were taken over by the Powell Duffryn Steam Coal Co., who remained owners until nationalisation in 1947. On 11 April 1860 the accident reports show that thirty-year-old collier Samuel Phillips was killed by a fall of roof at the Hafod Pit owned at the time by Rowlands & Calvert. Hafod No.2 Colliery ceased producing coal in 1930 and the Hafod No.1 Colliery in 1933.

Coed Cae Colliery Trehafod in 1900. The Owners Edward Mills opened the Coed Cae Colliery in 1850. In 1913 the manpower in the Coedcae was 556. On 18 May 1872 the accident reports show that fifteen-year-old collier R. Thomas was killed by a fall of coal. The Coed Cae Colliery ceased producing coal in 1929.

Llwyncelyn Colliery Porth in 1900. The height of the colliery was 290ft OD. The Colliery was sunk in 1851 by David James to the Rhondda No.2 and the Rhondda No.3 seams. The next owners were T. Edmunds and then the Lewis Merthyr Consolidated Collieries Ltd in 1891. On 1 December 1853 the accident reports show that nineteen-year-old haulier S.W. James Rees was killed by an explosion. Llwyncelin Colliery closed in 1895.

Cymmer Colliery, Porth, in 1920. George Insole started to develop the Cymmer mines in 1844 when he opened the South Cymmer Level in the Rhondda No.2 seam. In 1847 he sank the No.1 or Old Cymmer Pit, which struck the Rhondda No.3 seam at 1,104ft, the section of coal was 38in. In 1851 the Upper Cymmer Colliery was working at a depth of 372ft. In 1860 the Upper Cymmer Colliery was leased to T.C. Hinde, but was back in the hands of the Cymmer Colliery Co. in 1889. The New Cymmer Colliery was sunk in 1875 with the final sinkings starting in 1886 with two shafts being sunk to 384yds and later deepened to 435yds. The seams worked were: the Rhondda No.2, at a section of 36in; the Two-Feet-Nine, at 19in; the Six-Feet, at 109in; the Five-Feet, at 63in; the Rhondda No.3, at 38in; the Four-Feet, at 53in; and the Nine-Feet at 69in. In 1856 an explosion killed 114 men and boys. Cymmer Colliery closed in 1940.

Hinde's Upper Cymmer Colliery in 1910. The colliery was sunk in 1851 by Messrs Insole and later leased to T.C. Hinde, a Swansea coalowner. Water from old workings in the Rhondda No.3 seam caused the flooding of Tynewydd Colliery on 11 April 1877. On 13 August 1852 the accident reports show that thirty-five-year-old collier Aaron Rees was killed by a fall of roof at the Upper Cymmer Level owned by George Insole & Son and on 25 April 1853 the accident report also show that twenty-two-year-old collier Noah Llewellyn was killed by a fall of bell stone from the roof. Cymmer Colliery closed in 1940.

Tynewydd Colliery Porth in 1890. The colliery stood at 310ft OD. The colliery was sunk in 1852 to a depth of 270ft by the Troedyrhiw Coal Co. At approximately 4.00p.m. on Wednesday 11 April 1877 the Tynewydd Colliery was inundated with water from the old workings of the adjoining Hinde's Upper Cymmer Colliery. At the time of the inundation there were fourteen men in the pit, of whom four were unfortunately drowned and one killed by compressed air, leaving nine men imprisoned by the water; of this number four were released after eighteen hours imprisonment and five after nine days imprisonment.

Until the Tynewydd Colliery disaster the Albert Medal First and Second Class had been given only for bravery in saving life at sea. Then came Queen Victoria's announcement:

The Albert Medal, hitherto only bestowed for gallantry in saving life at sea, shall be extended to similar actions on land and that the first medals struck for this purpose shall be conferred on the heroic rescuers of the Welsh Miners.

The London Gazette published the list on 7 August 1877 as follows:

The Queen has been graciously pleased to confer the Albert Medal of the First Class on:
Daniel Thomas Colliery, proprietor, Brithwynydd Rhondda Valley South Wales
William Beith, mechanical engineer of Harris Navigation Colliery Quakers Yard South Wales
Isaac Pride, collier, Llwyncelyn Colliery Rhondda Valley South Wales
John William Howell, collier, Ynyshir Colliery Rhondda Valley South Wales.

The following is an account of the services in respect of which the decoration has been conferred:

On the 11 April 1877 the Tynewydd Colliery situated near Porth in the Rhondda Valley South Wales was inundated with water from the old workings of the adjoining Cymmer Colliery. At the time of the inundation there were fourteen men in the pit, of whom four were unfortunately drowned and one killed by compressed air, leaving nine men imprisoned by the water; of this number four were released after eighteen hours imprisonment and five after nine days imprisonment. It was in effecting the release of these latter five that those distinguished services were rendered which the conferring of the "Albert Medal of the First Class" is intended to recognise.

The rescuing operations consisted in driving through the barrier of coal thirty-eight yards in length, which intervened between the imprisoned men and the rescuers and kept back a large quantity of water and compressed air, this task was commenced on Monday the 16 April and was carried on until Thursday the 19 April without any great amount of danger being incurred by the rescuers, but about 1:00p.m. on that day, when only a few yards of barrier remained, the danger from an eruption of water, gas and compressed air was so great as to cause the colliers to falter. It was at this juncture that the above-mentioned four men volunteered to resume the rescuing operations, the danger of which had been greatly increased by an outburst of inflammable gas under great pressure and in such quantities as to extinguish the Davy lamps, which were being used. The danger from gas continued at intervals until 3:30a.m. on the following morning and from that time the above four men at great peril to their own lives continued the rescuing operations until 3:00p.m. when the five imprisoned men were safely released.

The Queen has been graciously pleased to confer the Albert Medal of the Second Class on:

George Albert, collier, Tynewydd Colliery Rhondda Valley South Wales
Charles Baynham, collier, Brithwynydd Colliery Rhondda Valley South Wales
Richard Hopkins, collier, Ynyshir Colliery Rhondda Valley South Wales
Richard Howells, overman, Tynewydd Colliery Rhondda Valley South Wales
Charles Oatridge, collier, Tynewydd Colliery Rhondda Valley South Wales
John Williams, collier, Pontypridd Colliery Rhondda Valley South Wales
Edward David, collier, Hafod Colliery Rhondda Valley South Wales
William Morgan, Hafod Colliery Rhondda Valley South Wales
David Rees, fireman, Tynewydd Colliery Rhondda Valley South Wales
Rees Thomas, collier, Tynewydd Colliery Rhondda Valley South Wales.

During the five days from the 16 April to the 20 April the above eleven men were at various times engaged in cutting through the barrier of coal separating them from the five imprisoned men and while exposing their own lives to the great danger which would have resulted from an outburst of compressed air and water and to the danger which actually existed from the presence of large quantities of inflammable gas, continued to perform their work until the five men were safely rescued.

The Queen has been graciously pleased to confer the Albert Medal of the Second Class on:

David Davies, colliery owner, Penrhiwfer, Rhondda Valley, South Wales
Thomas Jones, colliery owner, Ynyshir, Rhondda Valley, South Wales
Edmund Thomas, colliery owner, Llwyncelyn, Rhondda Valley, South Wales
James Thomas, colliery owner and manager, Tynewydd, Rhondda Valley, South Wales. [The part owner and manager was in the extraordinary position of being put up for an Albert Medal for bravery and being tried for manslaughter in connection with the same affair. However, the error was noted and his name removed from the list.]
Thomas Thomas, colliery manager, Ynyshir, Rhondda Valley, South Wales
Thomas Getrych Davies, colliery manager, Tylacoch, Rhondda Valley, South Wales
David Evans, colliery manager, Ferndale, Rhondda Valley, South Wales
David Jones, colliery manager, Cymmer Level, Rhondda Valley, South Wales
Henry Lewis, colliery manager, Energlyn Colliery, Monmouthshire
Isaiah Thomas, colliery manager, Brithwynydd Colliery, Rhondda Valley, South Wales
William Thomas, colliery manager, Resolven, Near Neath, Glamorganshire.

The following is an account of the services in respect of which the decoration has been conferred:

From Thursday the 12 April when the operations for the rescue were commenced until Friday the 20 April, when the intervening barrier of coal had been cut through and the imprisoned men released, the above-named eleven men were present at different times and while being of valuable service in the rescue, exposed their own lives to the great danger which would have attended an outburst of water and compressed air, or an explosion of the inflammable gas which at different times during the rescue escaped under great pressure and in dangerous quantities.

Tynewydd Colliery. The photograph includes the rescued men and the rescuers. The rescuing operations consisted in driving through the barrier of coal 38yds in length, which intervened between the imprisoned men and the rescuers and kept back a large quantity of water and compressed air, this task was commenced on 16 April 1877 and was carried on until 19 April 1877. Tynewydd colliery closed in 1901.

Troedyrhiw Colliery Porth in 1890. Troedyrhiw Colliery was the first pit to be sunk in the Rhondda Fach by L.J. Hadley in 1845 and was purchased by the Troedyrhiw Coal Co. in 1850. From 1875 it traded under the name Aberhondda Coal Co. and was locally known as Aberhondda Colliery. The shaft was only 88ft deep and worked the Rhondda No.3 seam. Aberhondda Colliery closed in 1901.

The Lady Lewis Colliery, Ynyshir, during sinking in 1903. The colliery was opened in 1904 by Lewis Merthyr Consolidated Collieries Ltd. The colliery stood at 361ft 6in OD, National Grid Ref. 02559233. Rhondda No.2 seam was sunk to 149ft 5in; Rhondda No.3 to 362ft 6in; Hafod to 525ft 3in; Lower Four-Feet to 1,070ft 7in; Six-Feet to 1,133ft; Upper Six-Feet to 1,214ft 11in; Lower Nine-Feet to 1,278ft 2in; Bute to 1,287ft 1in; Fault Yard to 1,294ft 6in, Upper and Middle Seven-Feet to 1,307ft 10in, Five-Feet to 1,404ft; and Gellideg to 1,426ft 6in. Lady Lewis Colliery was closed in 1950 by the NCB.

Left: Lady Lewis Colliery in the 1950s. The colliery was owned by the Powell Duffryn Steam Coal Co. prior to nationalisation in 1947. *Right:* Albert Isaacs, undermanager at the Lady Lewis Colliery in 1914. Mr Isaacs, formally of Aberhondda Road, worked at the Lady Lewis Colliery until its closure.

Ynyshir Colliery in 1903 – it stood at 388ft 6in OD, National Grid ref. 02559626. Ynyshir Colliery locally known as Jones's Pit was sunk by Messrs Shepherd & Evans in 1849 and seven years later it was purchased by Francis Crawshay to supply coal for his tinplate works at Treforest, the colliery employing about 100 men. In 1873 the colliery was owned by Thomas Jones of Maindy House, Ynyshir. The shaft was 198ft deep and the colliery worked the Rhondda No.2 seam at a section of 2ft 6in to 3ft, which supplied their own coking ovens. On Saturday 12 May 1877 there was an explosion in the Ynyshir Steam Coal Colliery owned by Daniel and James Thomas. At mid-day three men, John Howell, John Hopkins and Abraham Dodds, were driving a windway between the two shafts. They were drilling ahead and had holed into the passageway on the other side. Gas came through the holes made by the drills and burned in their Davy lamps. The lamps became hotter and hotter and Dodd suggested it was time to put them out. Hopkins assured him that there was no danger as he had been in the other passageway and it did not contain a dangerous quantity of gas. When the hole had been enlarged, Dodd put his head and arms through. At that moment there was a lurid flash and the explosion hurled Dodd back many yards. He felt his arms frying. Abraham Dodd lived in a cottage by the riverside at Ferndale where he suffered great pain, his face, arms and body looked like cooked meat. Abraham Dodd was a man with whom Isaac Pride took part in the final, most dangerous part of the rescue at Tynewydd Colliery. If any man deserved to be recognised that man was Dodd. Why does his name not appear? One can only guess at the explanation. Perhaps someone who reads these words may be in a position to clear the matter finally. It would give pleasure to another generation of Rhondda people to honour a man whose deeds were no less than those who were honoured by the Queen. The Forest Fach coal seam was at a depth of 149ft 11in with a thickness of 10in, and the Rhondda No.2 seam was at a depth of 174ft with a thickness of 2ft 10in. Ynyshir Colliery closed in 1909.

Standard Colliery Ynyshir in 1901 – it stood at 429ft 6in OD, National grid ref. 02449326. The Standard Colliery was sunk by James 'Siamps' Thomas in 1876 and by 1878 was producing 188,366tons of coal per year. Drift to 51ft, Rhondda No.2 coal seam was 229ft 11in; Two-Feet-Nine, 1,040ft 11in; Four-Feet, 1,096ft 8in; Upper Six-Feet, 1,163ft 2in; Lower Six-Feet, 1,187ft 6in; Upper Nine-Feet, 1,270ft 2in; Bute, 1,350ft 9in; Yard, 1,399ft 1in; Upper and Middle Seven-Feet, 1,413ft 7in; Five-Feet, 1,482ft 8in; Gellideg, 1,490ft; Garw, 1,570ft 11in, and sunk to 1,577ft 7in.

Left: James 'Siamps' Thomas born in Bedwellty in 1817 became an underground doorboy at the age of six; he also became a fireman, an overman and a colliery manager. *Right*: Standard Colliery in 1950. Filling drams underground at what is known as the 'Dump End'.

Standard Colliery Surface Workers in 1876. The Rhondda No.2 coal seam was worked extensively and the section of coal was 2ft 6in to 3ft. Siamps built Bryn Awel, situated opposite the
colliery. It is now a nursing home for the elderly.

Standard Colliery Surface Workers in the 1930s. In 1914 the Standard collieries were amalga-
mated with the United National collieries Co. Ltd who employed over 1,300 and producing
over 36,000tons of coal and later became part of the Ocean Coal Co. The colliery was acquired
by the NCB in 1947 and kept open for ventilation and pumping mine water only.

National Colliery Wattstown sketch. The colliery stood 453ft 6in OD, National Grid ref. 02129378. In the late 1870s two shafts were sunk at Pont-Y-Cwtch later to be known as Wattstown. In 1880 the pit was owned by the National Steam Coal Co. and Henry Lewis was the manager. The colliery was locally known as Cwtch and was sunk to the Six-Feet seam at a depth of 454yds. The Rhondda No.1 seam was also worked at a section of top coal 10in, clod 6in and coal 9in.

Left: A NCB lamp check for the National Colliery. The miners cap lamp and naked flame safety oil lamp were kept in the colliery lamp room. At the commencement of each shift every underground miner would report to the lamp room take his cap lamp and place a check on a hook above its place indicating that he was in work. He would then report to the Lodge – the name given to the office where officials gave their orders, and get his instructions. From there he would make his way to the top of the pit for his 'bond'. A bond is a name given to the pit cage when carrying men through the pit shaft. An official of the mine would check his lamps for safety. At the end of his shift he would replace his cap lamp to be charged, and his oil lamp to be cleaned refuelled and checked for safety. He would then remove his lamp check showing that he had arrived safely to the surface from the pit. In the event of an explosion it would instantly show who was still underground.

Left: Packer Walt Lovering, trainee supervisor, building a stone pack underground to support and control the roof following coal extraction at the K2 Training Face in the Six-Feet seam, 1968. *Right*: National Colliery No.2 Pit Bottom Upcast Shaft in 1968.

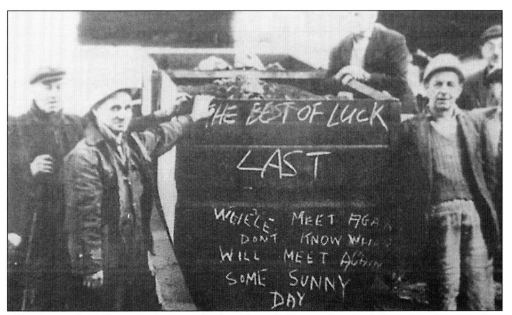

The National Colliery in 1968 on the last day of closure. On the left in the photograph is brakesman Cyril Banks. The downcast shaft was 17ft 6in diameter and the upcast shaft 14ft diameter. In 1900 the colliery employed 1,118 men. The first major explosion was on Friday 18 February 1887 and was caused by shot-firing, killing thirty-nine men and boys. The second explosion was on Tuesday 11 July 1905 killing 119 men and boys. This explosion was also caused by shotfiring. National Colliery was closed on 22 November 1968 by the NCB.

Tylorstown No.8 and No.9 Colliery Tylorstown in the 1920s. Sinking of No.8 Pit began in 1858. The venture failed after a short time and sinking was also twice interrupted by strikes. The working rites were then purchased by David Davis, but remained idle until 1892 when it was re-opened and sunk to the deeper seams. The colliery ceased coaling in 1935. No.9 Colliery was opened in 1907 by David Davis & Sons Ltd. The colliery was owned by the Powell Duffryn Steam Coal Co. prior to nationalisation in 1947. Tylorstown No.8 and No.9 Colliery was closed by the NCB on Friday 15 October 1960.

No.8 Colliery Cynllwyn-du South also known as Pontygwaith Colliery – it stood at 571ft 6in OD. National Grid Ref. 01069502.

Drift to 29ft 8in; Two-Feet-Nine at 1,223ft 3in; Four-Feet at 1,253ft 9in; Upper Six-Feet at 1,325ft 3in; Lower Six-Feet at 1,376ft 2in; Upper Nine-Feet (disturbed) at 1,525ft 11in; Lower Nine-Feet at 1,572ft 3in; Bute at 1,603ft 5in; Yard at 1,672ft 7in; Middle Seven-Feet at 1,707ft 10in; Five-Feet at 1,811ft 1in; and Gellideg at 1,819ft 2in.

Sinking began at Hen Bwll Waynes by Thomas Wayne of Cwmbach, Aberdare in 1858. The venture failed after a short time and sinking was also twice interrupted by strikes. The working rites were purchased by David Davis, but remained idle until 1892 when it was re-opened and sunk to the deeper seams.

Tylorstown No.9 Colliery Cynllwyn-du North – it stood at 580ft 6in OD. National Grid Ref. 01079507. Sunk 1904-07.

Drift to 39ft; Rhondda No.2 at 215ft 3in; Two-Feet-Nine at 1,232ft 6in; Four-Feet at 1,262ft 3in; Upper Six-Feet at 1,301ft 4in; Lower Six-Feet at 1,347ft; Upper Nine-Feet (disturbed) at 1,441ft 4in; Lower Nine-Feet at 1,486ft 1in; Bute at 1,525 feet and Yard at 1,651ft 1in.

No.9 Colliery was opened in 1907 by David Davis and Sons Ltd and closed by the NCB in 1960.

In 1914 No.8 and No.9 Collieries supplied coal to the British Admiralty. It was of an exceptionally good quality, fit for the service and met to the fullest extent requirements of marine boilers. In 1915 No.8 Pit employed 1,989 men and No.9 Pit employed 774 men.

To give an instance of the four Ferndale Colliery groups, the group comprising Nos 8 and 9 was particularly worthy of description. No.8 Pit was first sunk by Thomas Wayne in 1858 to the Six-Feet Seam at a depth of 1,301ft 4in and was originally called Pontygwaith Colliery and was also known locally as Cynllwyn-du Colliery. The Two-Feet-Nine and Four-Feet Seams, which lay above were won by cross-measure drivages so that the three seams might be raised from the same level.

Subsequently, No.9 Pit was opened in 1907 by David Davis and was 50yds to the North, and this pit was carried down to the Bute Seam at a depth of 1,525ft. Cross-measure drivages were again made to win the Yard Seam, lying 126ft below the Bute Seam, and also to the Five-Feet seam, lying 126ft below the Bute. Thus six seams had been won from this one pair of shafts. Ventilation was provided by an electrically driven fan capable of producing 300,000cu.ft of air per minute. Duplicate motors were provided for the fan each capable of producing the requisite circulation of air, so as to provide against any possible breakdown of this most essential factor in the safety of the colliery – the same safeguard being adopted at all the company's ventilating installations.

Electricity was very largely used as motive power. No.9 Pit was fitted with an electric winding engine plant, one of the first of any size used in South Wales. It was capable of raising up the shaft 1,400tons in seven hours from a depth of 512yds, the time taken for each wind being forty-five seconds.

All pumping and many of the underground main haulages were worked electrically. The subsidiary haulages, which were situated, further in the working were driven by blast (compressed air).

In No.8 shaft the coal was raised by the more usual steam driven winding engine, which raised two drams of coal per wind.

A carefully designed system of watering all main haulage roads for keeping down coal dust had been in force for many years. The water was brought down from the surface by pipes. These pipes were carried along all roads, with taps placed at intervals of 40yds; from the taps the water was sprayed over the roads. There were between thirty and forty miles of such pipes laid throughout the company's mines.

As a further safeguard against the danger of coal-dust explosions a stone-dust plant had been laid down. In this plant suitable shale was ground to the fineness of flour, and this fine dust was taken underground and distributed over the underground roadways in such a way that it mixed with the dangerous coal dust, which was thereby rendered non-flammable.

The long-wall system had been adopted for working the seams, some of the thinner seams being cut by machines. The use of machines for the getting of coal would increase in the future, as the thicker seams were being depleted, necessitating the working of the thin coals.

Large drams, each carrying 30 to 32cwt, were used for bringing the coal to the surface, and these were brought from the faces to the main haulages by powerful horses and small compressed-air engines.

The progressive policy of the company was again demonstrated in the early 1900s, when all the collieries were practically re-powered. This was carried out by the putting down of a large power station. Three Sulzer cross-compound horizontal engines, each capable of 2,500bhp and coupled to 1,600kW electric generators were first installed, then five years later a 5,000kW turbo-generator was added to the station. The necessary steam was provided by water-tuber boilers fitted with mechanical stokers.

The main power station was a well-constituted building. It was of brick, constructed on a steel frame, which sustained the whole weight of the roof and upper floors. The interior had walls of glazed white bricks with windows on sides and roofs and was splendidly lit. A travelling crane with a lifting power of 30tons was fitted overhead to cover the length of the building.

The average amount of electrical current distributed to the collieries was 13,000,000BThU per annum. This power was distributed by means of overhead lines at 6,600V to the several pits, where in sub-stations it was reduced to suitable voltage for the various motors working pumps, fans, surface and underground haulages, etc.

By the introduction of this power into the collieries, it was possible to dispense with much steam plant, boilers, etc. and thereby make a very large saving on the quantity of coal consumed at the collieries.

Tylorstown No.6 Colliery Pendyrus North – it stood at 625ft OD, National Grid ref. 01129589. Drift to 33ft 4in; Rhondda No.2, 123ft; Two-Nine, 972ft; Four-Feet, 999ft; Upper Six-Feet, 1,041ft; Lower Six-Feet, 1,086 ft; Upper Nine-Feet, 1,163ft; Lower Nine-Feet, 1,316ft 6in; Five-Feet, 1,380ft; Gellideg, 1,389ft and sunk to 1,392ft.

In 1872 the mineral rights of Pendyrus lands were bought by Alfred Tylor, after whom Tylorstown was named, and in 1873 the sinking of No.6 and No.7 shafts began. Great difficulties were encountered and it was not until 1876 that the steam coal seams were won. Coal was first despatched to Cardiff in January 1877 and subsequently, under the direction of Herbert Kirkhouse, the development of the Pendyrus Colliery was extremely rapid, output mounting from 3,252tons in 1877 to 241,061tons in 1893.

In 1914 No.6 and No.7 Collieries also supplied coal to the British Admiralty. It was of an exceptionally good quality, fit for the service and met to the fullest extent requirements of marine boilers.

In 1915 the No.6 pit employed 617 men and the No.7 pit employed 1,024 men. Coaling ceased in 1936 but the pits were retained for pumping and ventilation by vesting date 1 January 1947 and finally closed with No.8 and No.9 Colliery on 15 October 1960.

Tylorstown Colliery Explosion 28 January 1896.

The explosion which occurred at Tylorstown colliery on 28 January 1896 just after 5:30a.m. causing the deaths of fifty-seven miners brought to an end the brief respite from the accidents which had become so prevalent in the South Wales Coalfields during the late nineteenth century. Rumours spread like wildfire throughout the valley communities that a terrible disaster had occurred at Tylorstown. Wild claims were made which put the numbers of men trapped or buried as high as 700 and this naturally caused great panic among the relatives of the miners. One early newspaper report did little to calm the fears of the close, knit community: 'The angel of death had been at his dreaded task mowing down the colliers who were about to finish their work.'

The verdict delivered from the sixteen-man jury at the coroners Court, held at the Queens Hotel, Tylorstown, said.

> We are of the opinion that the cause of the explosion was the firing of a shot in gas, in the Daniel Williams Heading at No.8 Pit. That the air passing through the faces was charged with gas and the shot came in contact with the film of gas in Daniel Williams Road and that the explosion was also accelerated by coal dust. We also are of the opinion that no one now living is responsible for the explosion.

All the collieries were served by the Taff Vale Railway Co., which carried the coal direct to Cardiff or Penarth, or handed it over at Hafod Junction to the Barry Railway Co. for shipment at the Barry Docks.

The colliery was owned by the Powell Duffryn Steam Coal Co. prior to nationalisation in 1947. It ceased coaling in 1936 and closed with No.9 Colliery on Friday 15 October 1960 by the NCB.

Left: The Safety Lamp, which was used for light and testing for gas at the time of the explosion on 28 January 1896. Firedamp is a gas, which is found in most coalmines. When more than five parts of firedamp are mixed with ninety-five parts of air – that is to say, when the air contains over five per cent of firedamp – the mixture becomes explosive. *Right:* No.9 colliery mechanical engineer Glyn James, in the 1950s. Glyn made the spindle and keyway for Mardy Colliery pit wheel during its new development in 1950.

Tylorstown No.9 Colliery Electric Motors for driving the ventilation fans in 1900. Ventilation was provided by an electrically driven fan capable of producing 300,000cu.ft of air per minute. Duplicate motors were provided for the fan each capable of producing the requisite circulation of air, so as to provide against any possible breakdown of this most essential factor in the safety of the colliery. The same safeguard was adopted at all the company's ventilating installations.

Tylorstown No.8 and No.9 Miners Football Team in the 1950s. Before the miners were allowed to enter the bond (cage) they would be searched by the 'searcher' for any contraband, such as matches or cigarettes or anything that was likely to endanger life underground. Also checked were their oil lamps and battery lamps.

The Memorial for Tylorstown No.8 and No.9 Colliery was unveiled on 3 September 1999 by Peter Cloke of Groundwork, Merthyr, and Rhondda Cynon, Taff, and the Mid Fach River Care Group. Miners who worked at the colliery are, left to right: Gwyn Watkins, Ray Roberts, Essex Marden, Doug Jones, Ray Carter, David Owen, Garry Davies, Deryl Jones.

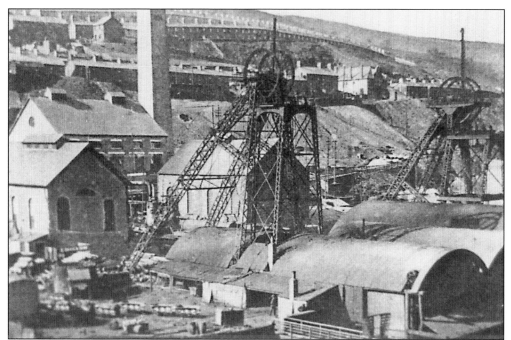

Tylorstown No.6 and No.7 Colliery in the early 1930s. In 1872 the mineral rights of Pendyrus lands were bought by Alfred Tylor, after whom Tylorstown was named and in 1873, sinking No.6 and No.7 shafts began. Great difficulties were encountered and it was not until 1876, at a depth of 333yds, that the steam coal seams were won. Coal was first despatched to Cardiff in January 1877 and subsequently, under the direction of Herbert Kirkhouse, the development of the Pendyrus Colliery was extremely rapid, output mounting from 3,252tons in 1877 to 241,061tons in 1893. In 1915 the No.6 Pit employed 617 men and the No.7 pit employed 1,024 men. Coaling ceased in 1936 and the pits were retained for pumping and ventilation by vesting date 1 January 1947 and was finally closed with No.8 and No.9 Colliery on 15 October 1960 by the NCB.

Tylorstown No.6 and No.7 Colliery Memorial in 1998. A memorial for Tylorstown No.6 and No.7 colliery began in January 1998 by the Mid Fach River Care Group. The opening cere-mony took place on May Day, 1998 and was unveiled by Dr E.I. Gwynne.

Ferndale No.1 and No.5 Colliery Ferndale in 1904. In August 1862, the first load of steam coal was sent from Ferndale to Cardiff and the industrial era of the Rhondda Fach had begun. The colliery was owned by the Powell Duffryn Steam Coal Co. prior to nationalisation in 1947. Ferndale No.1 and No.5 Colliery was closed on 29 August 1959 by the NCB.

Left: J.F. Davis (colliery secretary). 1797-1866. Coal was struck in No.1 Pit at a depth of 796ft 5in. Following this success, development work was speedily taken in hand. In 1866 the four sons of David Davis were brought into the venture and the firm of Messrs D. Davis & Sons was constituted. *Right:* F. Jacob JP (colliery manager). Immediately the steam coal seams were won, advertisements appeared in the South Wales press offering work under good conditions at Ferndale.

Ferndale No.1 Colliery, also known as Blaenllechau Colliery.

The colliery stood at 698ft OD, National Grid ref. 00239690. Drift to 53ft 6in; Two-Feet-Nine, 765ft 3in and Four-Feet at 796ft 5in.

Ferndale No.2 Colliery.

The colliery stood at 796ft OD, National Grid ref. 99039763. It was sunk in 1884. The Four-Feet seam at 667ft; Lower Six-Feet at 741ft; Upper Nine-Feet at 823ft; Lower Nine-Feet at 850ft; Yard at 923ft; Middle Seven-Feet at 961ft; Five-Feet at 1,008ft; Gellideg at 1,027ft and sunk to 1,050ft.

Ferndale Colliery No.3 Fan Pit.

The pit was 755ft OD, National Grid ref. 99679749. Lower Fan Pit had its fan installed in 1884, Middle Fan Pit was sunk in 1879 and Upper Fan Pit in 1875.

A detailed report on Blaenllechau Farm show how speculators' attention had been drawn to the mineral resources of the upper reaches of the Rhondda Fach in the mid-1840s. In November 1845, Thomas Thomas (alias Thomas Evans) wrote on the part of himself and his four brothers offering to give the Marquis of Bute refusal to 9 December 1845 to purchase the surface minerals and all rights of Blaenllechau Farm for £7,000. W.S. Clark advised Bute to offer £3,000, pointing out that the one bituminous seam worked on the property hitherto was only 2ft 6in thick and that the depth of the 'Lower Series' would be so great that little value could be attached to them. Bute did not buy the property and ten years elapsed before David Davis, the foremost coal pioneer of the Rhondda Fach, arrived in Blaenllechau.

In 1887 he leased the mineral rights of 500 acres of Blaenllechau lands from the Thomas brothers and bought their small, disused level. David Davis's first objective was the Rhondda No.3 seam, but his early mining difficulties were considerable. Transport, too, was a major problem for all machinery and materials had to be conveyed from the Aberdare Valley by horses, since the mountain track was too narrow for the passage of carts.

The coal seams in this area had never been proved and in 1858, after sinking to a depth of 115yds, the *Cambrian* reported:

> We learn that the pit of David Davis has passed the position of the No.3 vein, proving a continuity of the phenomenon of 'nip' on the east side of a line from Pontypridd to Pontwalby. Thus an immense tract of the valuable No.3 seam dwindled to nothing.

The enterprise was at a standstill.

Meanwhile, Lewis Davis, son of David Davis, made a survey across the mountains from Aberdare to Blaenllechau and advised his father to sink to a much greater depth to win the steam coal seams. In August 1859, after obtaining more favourable terms from the landlords, Davis recommended sinking. Eventually after much misgiving, on 14 June 1862, the Four-Feet seam was struck at the considerable depth of 796ft 5in and the efforts of David Davis, the promoter, Richard Pugh, the agent, and Cisle, the contractor, were duly rewarded. It was soon seen that this seam was superior in quality to the same seam found in the Aberdare Valley and a few years later, the shaft of the No.1 Pit was deepened to two new seams of equal importance, the Two-Feet-Nine and the Six-Feet. An immense mineral field had been opened up nearby and landlords Crawshay Bailey, De Winton Bruce and John Homfray, had to be 'remarkably cautious in their movements since every inch of property is so enhanced'. Meanwhile, the TVR was extended from the 'Little Pit' at Ynyshir to Blaenllechau and in August 1862, the first load of steam coal was sent from Ferndale to Cardiff. The industrial era of the Rhondda Fach had begun.

When sinking had commenced at Ferndale in 1857, there were but a few farmhouses in the locality – Blaenllechau and Nant-dyrys in the parish of Llanwynno, Ffaldau in the parish of Aberdare, Duffryn Sarfwch and Rhondda Fechan in the parish of Ystradyfodwg. Immediately the steam coal seams were won, advertisements appeared in the South Wales press offering work under good conditions at Ferndale. At first, the difficulty of accommodating the workers and their families was a serious one. The original sinkers, about forty in number, had been housed as one community in a single dwelling house 'Y Lluest', while the first miners and their families were accommodated in a large number of wooden huts called the 'Barracks'. Indeed, the *Times* reporter who visited Ferndale in November 1867 described how 'almost all the population of 800 was lodged in houses crudely built of wood, like American log huts'. It was in the 'seventies, when large numbers migrated into the district, that the huts were taken down and long terraces of stone houses were built by the colliery company to give shelter to this rapidly growing population.

Delta Davies, the first cashier of David Davis & Sons, changed the name Glynrhedynog to Ferndale in 1862.

At the Ferndale No.1 Pit output grew at an astonishing rate from 11,138tons in 1864 to 94,691tons in 1868. The brothers David Davis and Lewis Davis (previously in charge of the sales department at Cardiff) became partners with their father in 1866 and subsequently the firm was known as David Davis & Sons. On the sudden death of David Davis Sr on 20 May 1866, the control of the firm fell to the two sons. They were faced immediately with major crises on the occasion of two serious explosions, the first on 8 November 1867 with a loss of 178 lives and such grim statistics were put into context by one news correspondent who wrote:

> I doubt if any previous accident recorded in the annals of coal mining can have proved fatal to so large a proportion of the population of a district as this one. There are not more than two houses in the village that will not have to take on one or more dead bodies in the place of the living man or boy, which left there.

The second explosion was on 10 June 1869 when fifty-three miners were killed and at the resumption of the inquest on 1 July, the coroner addressed the jury:

> Again you have been summoned away from your homes and domestic duties, to discharge a most serious and important duty, another serious and appalling calamity has occurred in this district and caused grief and dismay to many households. It becomes our duty to investigate the circumstances and ascertain as far as possible the origin of the unfortunate occurrence.

Over the following days the court heard technical evidence presented by various pit officials. It was recorded that a fall had occurred on the day prior to the explosion. Several pockets of gas had been noted and marked by the fireman within the Duffryn area. Barometrical readings and ventilation information were also provided. During the second day of the hearing, the coroner was informed that another body had been recovered, bringing the total of dead recovered to forty-nine. The enquiry failed to reveal the exact cause of the explosion despite volumes of testimony from dozens of witnesses. The general consensus however was that gross negligence and lack of discipline by the general manager had contributed to most of the events that led up to the explosion and the verdict of the jury stated:

> We find that the deceased came to their death from an explosion of firedamp in the Ferndale Colliery, on the 10 June last; but we have not sufficient evidence to satisfy us as to where it arose.

In their summing up they added:

> We regret that we should have to investigate another explosion in this colliery so soon after the terrible catastrophe of 1867. We regret also that the suggestions of the jury on that occasion have not all been fully carried out by the manager and other officers of the pit.

These disasters, in such rapid succession, threatened ruin to the mining enterprise. For a time, Ferndale had a bad name as a bad place and the shadow of death seemed to rest over the valley. People were drifting away and many prophesied that, to get men to work there again would be a difficulty, if not impossibility. In his report on the explosion of 1867, HM Inspector, Thomas Wales, described Ferndale No.1 Pit as 'one of the best ventilated and best managed pits under my supervision! But Lewis Davis (1829-1888), the second founder of the Ferndale enterprise, decided to improve ventilation further by opening a new shaft Ferndale No.2 Pit in 1870 about a mile higher up the valley. The new venture was so successful that in the flourishing seventies, the mineral taking was extended and several new shafts were opened. On 3 May 1890, the Ferndale concern became a limited company, which immediately purchased the Bodringallt Colliery in the Rhondda Fawr (subsequently Ferndale No.3 Pit). Bodringallt Colliery was opened in 1864 by Warner, Simpson & Co., Ystrad and by vesting date 1 January 1947 was retained for ventilation. The colliery closed in 1959 along with Ferndale No.1 and No.5 Pits.

By 1914, the Ferndale mineral property embraced all the seams lying under a surface area of between six and seven square miles, covering on continuous coal-taking extending from the Rhondda Fach to the Rhondda Fawr, with their northern boundary near Mardy and their southern boundary at Tylorstown worked by nine winding shafts. In the same year, 5,654 men were employed, producing an output of 1,750,000tons. From the small beginnings of 1862 had grown one of the major colliery enterprises in the South Wales Coalfield.

Above: The Lamp Check belonged to collier Lewis 'Penzance' Williams formally of 2 Mountain Row Blaenllechau. *Right:* Master John Davies 1899-1965 had just completed his first days work underground at Ferndale No.1 Colliery at the age of twelve. He had to pass the 'Labour Exam' before acquiring a job as a miner.

Ferndale Colliery Officials in 1897. On 21 March 1868 the accident reports show that thirty-four-year-old collier J. Beecher was killed by a fall of roof and on 23 April 1868 the accident reports show that thirteen-year-old doorboy H. Josephs was killed by a journey of drams.

The Gold Medals were awarded to Griffiths Thomas 'Griff y Gof' Williams for splicing and capping at the Ferndale horse show in 1906. If coal was King in the valleys then the horse was the Prince, heavily relied on by the collieries, tradesmen and professional people for transport and haulage, the better off even using them for leisure activities.

 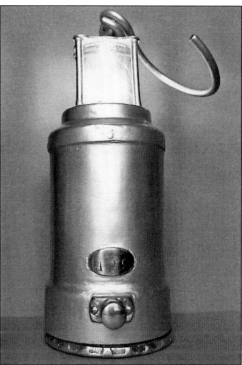

Left: Two miners prepared for work at Ferndale Colliery in 1907. The naked flame safety lamp was in use. The young miner has a naked flame safety lamp in his right hand, a Tommy Box (food box) under his left arm and he is also carrying a 3pt drinking water Jack in his left hand. *Right:* An Oldham lighthouse type safety battery operated lamp used by Mathew Rossiter at Ferndale No.1 Pit. Mathew left school at twelve years of age and started work at Ferndale No.1 Colliery, he served his country as a soldier in the Second World War, worked in the building trade for six months and returned to the pits until his retirement in 1968 at sixty-five years of age. He was a member of the Tylorstown Brass Band and his last pit of employment was Mardy.

Ferndale Colliery Electric House in 1908. On 21 May 1868 the accident reports show that thirty-eight-year-old collier D. Davies was killed by a fall of roof. On 15 January 1872 the accident reports show that twenty-nine-year-old collier P.W. Richards was killed by a journey of drams.

Ferndale No.1 Colliery Pit Bottom Main Haulage in 1908. The development work, which had been taken in hand at Ferndale, resulted in sharply increasing production until 1870 when it reached the satisfactory total of 239,204tons, a figure, which gave Ferndale a leading rank amongst South Wales Colliery undertakings.

The Drinking Mug belonging to Islwyn Thomas of Pentre Road Maerdy was presented to the school children of the area to commemorate the coming of age of Lewis Fredrick Davis of Ferndale on his twentieth birthday, 11 July 1913. Islwyns' father Sam was a winder at Mardy Colliery. The rising and lowering of the cage is, controlled by a winder (winding engine man) who is stationed in the winding house opposite the pit shaft area. Because of the risk to lives when operating the huge drum of the winding engine the area was a no-go area except for the men who actually worked there as one slip of concentration could spell disaster. Contact with the pit was made through a method of signals between the winder, hitcher and the banksman. The banksman had a cabin on the pit top and controlled the movement of the cage up and down the shaft. He in turn had contact through a set of signals underground from men known as hitchers, (onsetters). The hitcher would then signal the banksman who would transfer the signal to the winder before the cage moved.

Lord Roseberry Champion Colliery Horse at Ferndale Colliery in 1912. On 7 January 1888 the accident reports show that twenty-eight year-old haulier Rob Collard and eighteen-year-old haulier John Davies were killed underground by going up an engine plane with their horses, while a journey was coming down, a shackle broke and they were run over by three runaway drams. In 1916 the output of coal from Nos 1, 2, 3, 4, 5, 6, 7, 8 and 9 Collieries was 1,900,000tons.

Above: Ferndale Colliery at full production in the 1920s. The miner fourth from the left has a bundle of firewood. *Right:* Ferndale Colliery in 1930 with the Gas Storage Tank, the Lower School and Christ Church in the background. Ferndale No.1 and No.5 Colliery was closed on 29 August 1959 by the NCB.

The Unveiling of the Memorial for the Ferndale Collieries on Friday 15 July 1988. In memory of the 178 miners who lost their lives on 8 November 1867 and the fifty-three miners who lost their lives on 10 June 1869 at Ferndale No.1 Pit. Buried beneath the memorial in a steel 'time capsule' is a scroll inscribed with all the names of the 231 miners who died in the Ferndale Colliery explosions.

Blaenllechau Level in 1910. The mine worked the Rhondda No.2 seam at a section of 2ft 6in, was the only commercially worked level in the Rhondda Fach and the owners were David Davis & Sons. The method of working at this level was by pillar and stall. A main heading was driven from the level into the seam. Then at intervals, along one or both sides of this main heading, smaller headings were turned off at right angles. From these cross headings, stalls were cut at intervals and it was by the excavation of these stalls that the bulk of the coal was won. As the seam was penetrated, square, or almost square, pillars of coal were left standing about every ten yards in order to support the roof. In size, these pillars depended on the depth of the working, the hardness of the seam and the strength of the roof and floor. Blaenllechau level was driven in approximately 500yds, and then it was faced with a 14ft fault completely losing the seam of coal. Blaenllechau level closed on 20 September 1913.

Ferndale No.2 and No.4 Colliery in 1900. The colliery locally known as Ffaldau Pits was sunk in 1870 by David Davis & Sons. The Four-Feet was at a depth of 667ft; Lower Six-Feet at 741ft; Upper Nine-Feet at 823ft; Lower Nine-Feet at 850ft; Yard at 923ft; Middle Seven-Feet at 961ft; Five-Feet at 1,008ft; Gellideg at 1,027ft and sunk to 1,050ft. Ferndale No.2 and No.4 Colliery closed in 1930.

Ferndale No.2 and No.4 Colliery Timbermen with their Tŷ Gwyn hatchets in 1897. One of the better and favourite hatchets, which were used, was the Y Bwyall Tŷ Gwyn (the white house hatchet) and the timbermen always kept them sharp as razor blades. The miners in the photograph stand timber (pit props) underground known as the Collar and Arms using the Welsh Notch at the joints.

Ferndale Coal on its way to the Grande Canary in 1920. The Ferndale Collieries also supplied coal to the British Admiralty. It was of an exceptionally good quality, fit for the service and met to the fullest extent requirements of marine boilers.

Ferndale No.2 and No.4 Colliery Workshop in 1920. Whilst most of the leading Welsh colliery companies affected their own wagon repairs, Ferndale had gone a step further, for not only did they do their own repair work, but they also built their own wagons. To perform this task a fine works had been erected at No.2 and No.4 Pits. They were equipped on the most modern lines with the best machinery obtainable and were run by electrical power. The main building of the wagon works was 240ft by 65ft with a height of 22ft. Railway lines ran the length of the building. They were able to turn out ten new wagons per week. They also built their own steel drams, which were used underground, in a further shop especially erected for the purpose.

Mardy No.1 and No.2 Colliery Maerdy in the 1880s. Mardy Colliery No.1 Pit stood at 949ft OD, National Grid ref. 97369885.

In 1875 Mardy No.1 Pit was sunk by contractors Messrs Robert Jones & Sons to the Abergorki seam and a year later in 1876 Mardy No.2 Pit was also sunk to the Abergorki seam, in 1876 the winding engine man was Daniel 'Eos Dar' Evans from Station Terrace, he was also the winding engine man when the explosion claimed the lives of eighty-one men and boys on 23 December 1885, his crossing 'Butty' was Morgan 'Engineer' Davies. Top quality dry steam coal was produced in 1877 by Lockets-Merthyr Collieries 1894 Ltd. William Thomas (engineer), James Miles (manager), William Edwards (cashier) and Taliesin E. Richards (surveyor). In 1906 Lockets-Merthyr Collieries Ltd Taliesin E. Richards (manager & engineer); William Edwards (cashier) and Arvon Price (surveyor).

The Marquis of Bute declined the purchase of the 999-acre land and mineral rights of Maerdy Farm in 1847 and it was purchased in 1873 for £122,000, by Mordecai Jones, additional capital was required for the hazardous task of sinking, he then formed a partnership with Wheatley Cobb of Brecon.

The early career of Mr Jones was as a coal merchant at Brecon and his first public undertaking of any account was the purchase of Abergavenny Gas Works, in connection with Mr Kirk.

In the year 1866 Dr Roberts and he leased the coal area of Nantmelyn in the Cwmdare Valley Aberdare, from the Gwynne-Holford family and entered upon the hazardous speculation of sinking for coal. But in this, as in the principal aims of his life, he was most successful and before twelve months had passed he struck coal. This proved a most valuable property, turning out 500-600tons daily and Mrs Roberts, widow of Dr Roberts, obtained as her share on retirement £22,000.

He entered upon the Mardy Pit enterprise with vigour. It was a bleak waste amongst the Rhondda hills, with only a lone farmhouse to be seen. Thanks to his enterprise, the great tract became a populous district, a whole township of houses, churches and chapels, met the eye and its history, up to the great tragedy of 1885, had been a bright and progressive one.

In sinking he was again fortunate; in 1875 Mardy No.1 Pit was sunk to the Abergorki seam and a year later in 1876 Mardy No.2 Pit was sunk. Top quality dry steam was produced in 1877 and the first truck, gaily decorated with flags, was sent into Brecon on the day of his taking the post of High Sheriff for the county.

He was offered £12,000 per annum for a tract of land each side the river, but refused it, spent £72,000 and eventually sold it for £10,000.

In this Mardy enterprise Mr Cobb, of Brecon, who, in trading enterprise and in archaeological effort and castle restoration, deserves special mention and honour, joined him.

Failing health led to the leasing of the Mardy Colliery, not the estate, to Mr Locket (and others), descendant of Mr Locket of the Four-Feet coal history and its value was shown by the fact that the plant alone was estimated at £55,000.

This was his last great speculation, and though his mind retained its robustness and his sympathetic nature was shown by unceasing acts of good will and charity, the body rapidly faded and on the 30 August 1880, he died.

In addition to his colliery engagements, he was chairman of Brecon Gas Works from the commencement, had been mayor, was deputy lieutenant of his county and JP for three counties. From youth he was a member of the Calvinistic Methodists and materially assisted in founding a Welsh and an English chapel in Brecon. He was superintendent of the Sunday school and deacon and energetic in the cause of moral and religious effort.

He had a lengthened career, but it was characterised by remarkable success. In his youth, in early trading speculation, he was one of the fortunate. Whatever he touched turned to gold. He was energetic to a degree, his perseverance undaunted. In habits, plain, in all positions taken by him, unassuming, sober and discreet, unaffected by success. Perhaps the tribute of a widow at his last resting place in Brecon was as fitting as it was brief – 'A spotless life from the cradle to the grave.'

The railway from Mardy to Ferndale was opened and owned privately by Mordecai Jones in 1877; at Ferndale the Taff Vale Railway owned the railway and the coal was transported to Cardiff Docks. In 1878 the No.1 Pit was deepened to the rich steam coal seams of the Two-Feet-Nine, the Four-Feet and the Six-Feet seams, the colliery was leased to Locket & Co., who then became Lockets-Merthyr Steam Coal Co. in 1879.

The explosion at Mardy No.1 and No.2 Colliery on Wednesday 23 December 1885 at quarter to three in the afternoon claimed the following eighty-one men and boys lives.

In everlasting memory

1. Collier. Joseph Baber (17), of 61 Mardy Road, Mardy. Single.
2. Haulier. John Bevan (25), of 28 Hill Street, Mardy. Single.
3. Spragger. Arthur Boozay (21), of 5 Oxford Street, Mardy. Single.
4. Collier. David Bowen (18), of 21 Cemetery Road, Treorchy. Single.
5. Collier. John Collins (40), of 109 Mardy Road, Mardy. Single.
6. Collier. Evan Davies (28), of 6 Rowley Terrace, Mardy. Married with one child.
7. Collier. Evans Davies (19), of 8 Hill Street, Mardy. Single
8. Repairer. Isaac Davies (33), of 4 Wrgant Place, Mardy. Married with two children.
9. Collier boy. John Davies (17), of 113 Mardy Road, Mardy. Single.
10. Mason. Lewis Davies (32), of 1 Mardy Road, Mardy. Married with three children.
11. Collier. Thomas Davies (49), of 1 Thomas Street, Mardy. Married with five children.
12. Collier boy. Thomas Davies (13), of 1 Thomas Street, Mardy. Single.
13. Collier. William Davies (25), of 35 Ferndale Road, Tylorstown. Married with two children.
14. Contractor. Edward Edwards (52), of 42 Oxford Street, Mardy. Married with nine children.
15. Stoneman. Edward Edwards (16), of 42 Oxford Street, Mardy. Single.
16. Collier Boy. John Edwards (13) of 22 Thomas Street, Mardy. Single.
17. Collier Boy. David Evans (16), of 85 Mardy Road, Mardy. Single.

18. Labourer. John Evans (55), of 2 Rowley Terrace, Mardy. Married with three children.
19. Fireman. John Evans (45), of 32 North Road, Ferndale. Married with six children.
20. Collier. John Evans (25), of 6 Rowley Terrace, Mardy. Single.
21. Collier. Richard Evans (24), of 120 Mardy Road, Mardy. Single.
22. Collier. Thomas Evans (26), of 21 Pentre Road, Mardy. Married with three children.
23. Haulier. Thomas Evans (26), of 17 Pentre Road, Mardy. Widower with one child.
24. Haulier. Robert Griffiths (34), of 7 Hill Street, Mardy. Married with four children.
25. Collier. William Griffiths (16), of 69 Oxford Street, Mardy. Single.
26. Collier. William Harries (29), of 43 Mardy Road, Mardy. Married with four children.
27. Collier. John Heard (22), of 28 Pentre Road, Mardy. Single.
28. Spragger. Ephraim Hughes (20), of 52 Mardy Road, Mardy. Single.
29. Shackler. Thomas Hughes (33), of 5 Ceridwen Street, Mardy. Married with two children.
30. Hitcher. Phillip Hutchins (35), of 90 Mardy Road, Mardy. Married with three children.
31. Haulier. Henry Isaac (23), of 101 Mardy Road, Mardy. Single.
32. Collier. Evan James (21), of 18 Pentre Road, Mardy. Married.
33. Cogman. Thomas Jenkins (25), of 52 Mardy Road, Mardy. Single.
34. Miner. David Jones (20), of 56 Mardy Road, Mardy. Single.
35. Logman. David Jones (59), of 1 Pentre Road, Mardy. Married with eight children.
36. Timberman. David Jones (55), of 35 Pentre Road, Mardy. Married with one child.
37. Collier. David Jones (27), of 5 Oxford Street, Mardy. Married.
38. Collier. David Jones (25), of 23 Thomas Street, Mardy. Married with two children.
39. Collier. Isaac Jones (20), of 12 Thomas Street, Mardy. Single.
40. Collier. John Jones (42), of 11 Hill Street, Mardy. Married with four children.
41. Collier Boy. William Jones (12), of 11 Hill Street, Mardy. Single.
42. Bratticeman. John D. Jones (51), of 74 Mardy Road, Mardy. Married with one child.
43. Miner. Joseph Jones (40), of 82 Mardy Road, Mardy. Single.
44. Collier Boy. William Jones (16), of 21 Thomas Street, Mardy. Single.
45. Collier. David Lake (35), of 40 Pentre Road, Mardy. Single.
46. Collier. David Lewis (40), of 53 Mardy Road, Mardy. Widower with four children.
47. Collier. John Lewis (19), of 2 David Street, Ferndale. Single.
48. Collier. Richard Lewis (46), of 6 North Terrace, Mardy. Widower with one child.
49. Labourer. James Loxton (28), of 13 Pentre Road, Mardy. Single.
50. Collier. Edmund Morgan (27), of 52 Pentre Road, Mardy. Married.
51. Haulier. Gomer Morgan (21), of 100 Mardy Road, Mardy. Single.
52. Haulier. John Morgan (17), of 19 Hill Street, Mardy. Single.
53. Hitcher. James Parry (29), of 107 Mardy Road, Mardy. Married with one child.
54. Roadman. Benjamin Phillips (40), of 2 Pit Row, Ferndale. Married with six children.
55. Mason. David Phillips (50), of 11 Thomas Street, Mardy. Married with five children.
56. Mason. Meshach Phillips (33), of 75 Oxford Street, Mardy. Married.
57. Haulier. Thomas Phillips (21), of 11 Thomas Street, Mardy. Single.
58. Hitcher. John Powell (23), of 7 Rowley Terrace, Mardy. Single.
59. Collier. Owen Powell (28), of 20 Llewelyn Street, Pontygwaith. Married with two children.
60. Collier. Evan Pugh (17), of 32 Oxford Street, Mardy. Single.
61. Hitcher. Henry Pullen (23), of 25 Mardy Road, Mardy. Single.
62. Labourer. Phillip Richards (46), of 83 Mardy Road, Mardy. Married with six children.
63. Roadman. Evan Roberts (18), of 23 North Terrace, Mardy. Single.
64. Collier. David Rowlands (27), of 19 Oxford Street, Mardy. Married with three children.
65. Labourer. Griffith Scourfield (19), of 86 Mardy Road, Mardy. Single.
66. Collier. Joseph Spiller (22), of 10 Mardy Road, Mardy. Single.
67. Haulier. Michael Stokes (17), of 1 Mardy Huts, Mardy. Single.
68. Labourer. James Sutton (28), of 13 Pentre Road, Mardy. Single.
69. Collier. David Thomas (19), of 4 Mardy Huts, Mardy. Single.

70. Rider. Edward Thomas (23), of 24 Pentre Road, Mardy. Married with one child.
71. Collier. James Thomas (24), of 108 Mardy Road, Mardy. Married.
72. Miner. John Henry Thomas (23), of 9 Thomas Street, Mardy. Single.
73. Collier. Thomas Thomas (24), of 29 Pentre Road, Mardy. Single.
74. Collier. William Thomas (19), of 33 Pentre Road, Mardy. Single.
75. Miner. Owen Tudor (32), of 2 Rowley Terrace, Mardy. Married with three children.
76. Door boy. Morgan Watkins (14), of 6 Oxford Street, Mardy. Single.
77. Haulier. Thomas Watkins (17), of 6 Oxford Street, Mardy. Single.
78. Overman. Daniel Williams (43), of 33 North Road, Ferndale. Married with seven children.
79. Collier. John Williams (25), of 52 Pentre Road, Mardy. Single.
80. Roadman. Levi Williams (60), of 89 Mardy Road, Mardy. Married with three children.
81. Miner. William Williams (30), of 13 North Terrace, Mardy. Married.

The injured were:

Richard Davies, 28 Ceridwen Street, Mardy, received serious burns to his head, face, hands and body.
John Jones, 90 Mardy Road, Mardy, had burns on his head, face and hands, and made a good recovery.
Mr. Lewis, 127 Mardy Road, Mardy, had slight burns on his hands and face.
Gomer Rees, The Huts, Mardy, had very serious burns on his head, face, hands and body.
John Henry Thomas (23), of 9 Thomas Street, Mardy, received serious burns.
John Williams, 24 Oxford Street, Mardy; had very serious burns to his head, face, hands and body.

Once again a sad reminder of the true price of coal.

The naked flame Comet lamp caused the explosion at Mardy No.1 and No.2 Colliery just before Christmas on Wednesday 23 December 1885 killing eighty-one men and boys. *They take us from our cradles and they work us to death.*

Mardy No.1 and No.2 Colliery Rescue Team. When the rescue team reached the underground air doors, lying face down was a young lad and when they moved his body they found his little dog called 'try', his faithful friend and loving companion, the boy, David Evans, had tried to shield his little friend from the horrific event.

Left: Mr Robert Jones survivor of the 1885 explosion with his family. There were thirty-eight horses underground at the time of the explosion, but only fifteen survived. Jack and Jerry, two Welsh ponies, were not found until Boxing Day and when brought together made a terrible fuss of each other. Finally being brought to the surface and led to green pastures.

Left, left to right: Mardy Colliery Miners in 1918. Llew Morgan, young Will 'Mwch' Morgan, Twm Morgan formally of 60 Pentre Road Maerdy. *Right:* Mr Davies worked underground for seventy-three years and by so doing earned himself a place in the Guinness Book of Records. He started work underground at the age of seven and retired at the age of eighty. His record of achievement will never be broken. *Left to right, back row:* Mary Thomas, Olwen Williams. *Sitting:* Mrs and Mr David Davies. *Front, standing:* Miss Glenys Williams (Mrs Glenys Edwards). At North Terrace Maerdy in 1925.

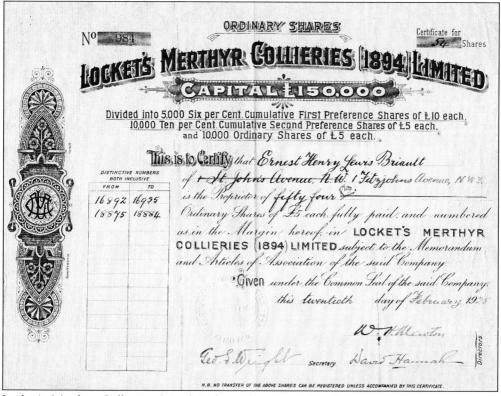

Locket's Merthyr Collieries (1894) Ltd Certificate for fifty-four shares 12 February 1925. Output for Mardy No.1 and No.2 Colliery. In 1879 the output was 29,337tons, in 1882 the output was 98,000tons and in 1883 the output was 160,000tons. On the 19 Jan 1896 Oil Girl Louisa Thomas age twenty-two was killed by a dram running wild down the surface incline.

Mardy No.1 and No.2 Colliery Ambulance Brigade in the 1920s, with Dr S. Glanville Morris Chief Surgeon for the Mardy collieries and compiler of the first addition of the First Aid Book. Mardy No.1 Squad became famous for the holders of the Sir C. Warren's Rhondda Shield, the Glamorgan County Shield and the Provincial White Horse Shield, besides being holder of three champion cups and eight gold and silver medals.

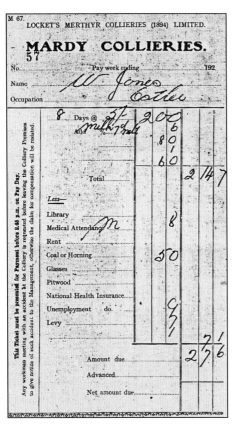

Left: Ostler William Jones Last Pay Docket. Mardy No.1 and No.2 Colliery was the scene of a tragedy in 1931, when three men, whose task was to prepare the pit for resumption of work after a weekend, lost their lives. The reason for this accident was that the bridle had been left on for raising the water from the sump. The winder, David Thomas of 9 Station Terrace, Maerdy, did not realise this and released the cage. The cage went straight into the sump, drowning its occupants. A very large funeral took place at Maerdy Cemetery on Thursday 18 August 1931 for ostlers, David Davies and Williams Jones. The third ostler, John Thomas, was also a farrier and was buried at Aberdare Cemetery on 31 August 1931. Mardy No.1 and No.2 Colliery was closed in 1940 by the Powell Duffryn Steam Coal Co.

Below: Mardy No.1 and No.2 Colliery during site reclamation in September 1992, which included filling and making safe both shafts, landscaping the colliery site and the tip. Mardy No.1 and No.2 Colliery was once one of fity-three collieries in the Rhondda, which at their peak production in 1913 produced nearly 10m tons of saleable coal. At that time, a trainload of coal containing 500tons left the Rhondda every ten minutes of the working day and more than 40,000 miners were employed in the Rhondda pits at the time.

Mardy No.3 and No.4 Colliery, Maerdy, in December 1949 before redevelopment. Mardy No.3 Pit stood at 1,064ft OD 6 in SS 99 North East, Glamorgan, 18 North West. It was sited 1,870yds north-west of Maerdy railway station. National Grid ref. 96379987.

Drift to 34ft 11in, Gorllwyn at 779ft 8in; Two-Feet-Nine at 1,022ft 7in; Four-Feet at 1,070ft 5in; Upper-Six-Feet at 1,087ft 1in; Lower-Six-Feet at 1,142ft 10in; Red-Vein at 1,160ft; Nine-Feet at 1,235ft 6in; Bute at 1,279ft 8in; Yard at 1,359ft 11in; Upper and Middle Seven-Feet at 1,373ft 1in; Gellideg at 1,455ft 5in. Sunk to 1,499ft 4in.

Mardy No.3 Pit was opened in 1893 and No.4 Pit opened in 1914 by Lockets-Merthyr Steam Coal Co.

1 January 1947 and the coming of nationalisation. Mardy Colliery was placed in the NCB's South Western Divisions, No.4 (Aberdare Area) and at that time employed five men underground and ten men on the surface on a maintenance basis. In 1948 plans were made for Mardy Colliery to be the first redeveloped colliery in South Wales at a cost of £5 million and would be linked underground with Bwllfa No.1 Colliery in the Cynon Valley.

In 1954 the new mine was fully operational and employed 185 men on the surface and 890 men underground working the Two-Feet-Nine, Four-Feet and Six-Feet seams, while the Bwllfa section worked the Five-Feet seam. Development of the mine was still continuing into the early 1960s when the contractors, Cementation, employed sixty-four men at Mardy working on staple shafts, headings and drivages.

The official opening of the redeveloped Mardy No.3 and No.4 Colliery took place on Saturday 28 August 1954 and Mr A.L. Horner; the general secretary of the NUM conducted the ceremony. The colliery manager was Mr D.M. 'The hooker' James.

The official opening of the redeveloped Bwllfa No.1 Colliery was opened on Saturday 8 January 1955 and Mr H. Watkins who had the longest unbroken service at Bwllfa Collieries, conducted the ceremony. The underground manager of Bwllfa was Mr A. Lewis.

Nantmelyn Pit in the Cynon Valley was also linked to Mardy Colliery and was used for pumping mine water. Mordecai Jones of Morgannwg House, Brecon, opened Nantmelyn pit to the Four-Feet seam in 1866.

Mardy No.3 and No.4 Colliery in September 1950 during redevelopment. Maerdy No.3 Pit at the head of the Rhondda Fach was sunk in 1893 at a dept of 500yds and No.4 was sunk in 1914 at a depth of 428yds by Lockets-Merthyr Steam Coal Co. In 1948 plans were made for Mardy to be the first redeveloped colliery in South Wales at a cost of £5 million and would be linked underground with Bwllfa No.1 Colliery in the Cynon Valley.

Mardy No.4 Colliery Blue Pit Bottom in March 1951. Large reserves of coal were still to be worked at Mardy Colliery for an estimated 100 years. A promise made, but once again broken when the closure of last day of production at colliery came on Thursday 20 December 1990.

Mardy No.3 Red Pit Bottom with hitcher (onsetter) Idris 'Spike' Price. The new roadways extended for almost a mile in a northerly direction from Mardy and more than a mile southwest from Bwllfa. They met at an angle and the drivage was then continued northward. But it was not just one roadway from each colliery. In fact, there were three roadways, the Yellow, Red and Blue Horizons all parallel with each other at different levels.

Driving the Red Horizon in March 1951. The project was scheduled to reach a maximum output of 4,000tons a day, or approximately 1m tons per annum, by the early 1960's. As was apparent on the surface where new administrative offices, workmen's canteens, pithead baths, medical centre, electrical winding-engine house, workshops, coal preparation plant, etc., had been erected, the derelict scene of 1940-1949 had been completely trans-formed.

Bwllfa Turn Red Horizon in November 1951. The project envisaged a completely modern colliery on the site of the old Mardy Nos 3 and 4 pits to work extensive reserves calculated at 1m tons – sufficient to last 100 years – of sub-bituminous, low volatile, dry steam coal. The total number of men required was estimated to be 2,800. The scheme provided, the continuation of employment of men from the Bwllfa Pits (where separate pithead amenities had been provided for the men as they enter or leave the pits), and the opportunity of employment for the men of the Ferndale (closed on 29 August 1959 by the NCB) and Tylorstown Collieries (closed on 15 October 1960) by the NCB.

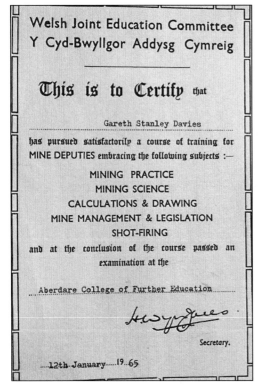

Left: Certificate for mining practice, mining science, calculations and drawing, mine management and legislation and shot-firing awarded to Gareth 'Gary' Stanley Davies 12 January 1965. *Above:* Dai 'Safety' Jones (colliery safety officer) with Essex Marden fireman (colliery official) at the Red Horizon Dump End in the 1970s.

Preparing for shot-firing in the 1970s by permitted explosives only. The person must be qualified with a mines certificate, authorised and appointed in writing by the manager. The shot-firer's equipment include: an approved safety lamp for all firedamp testing, which is imperative and such lamps have a re-lighting device and are adjustable by the user to admit air at the top of the lamp only when actually testing; an approved electric cap lamp, both must be locked and he must examine them before entering the mine; and a locked case with detonators only. He should check the number before leaving the magazine and keep the case locked on his person, key to lock

detonator case, key to the exploder kept fastened to the person, a pricker for making a hole in the primer cartridge without opening it. This tool must be of copper or brass, a secure canister containing no more than 5lb of explosive of one kind only; an efficient and suitable exploder; a copper scraper to clean out the shot-hole; a copper breakfinder to detect lateral and longitudinal breaks in the shot-hole; a wooden rammer, no iron or steel must be used for any pricker, stemmer, scraper or breakfinder. The cable should be at least 25yds long and must not be allowed to touch power or lighting circuits and must be insulated and protected. A pocketknife for baring the wire of the cable ends and stone dust the whole neighbourhood of the shot should be thoroughly covered with fresh incombustible dust before firing for a radius of five yards and continuous with any road within 10yds of the shot. Before firing shots, a shotfirer must test for gas, see that sentries are posted and that everyone has withdrawn from that zone and he must take proper shelter in a manhole.

Left: Mardy Colliery Pithead Baths in the 1970s.

Mardy NUM Lodge Committee in 1973. *Left to right, back row:* Jerry Condon, Will Sly, Brian, Vincent, Alan Ivor 'Masum' Jones, Jack Stocks, Tommy Rogers, J. Trebey, John Cox, John Podmore, Dai Bowen, Trevor Roberts, Alan Carter. *Front row:* Eddie Davies (compensation secretary), Harry Bugg Bwllfa (compensation secretary), Haydn Mathews (secretary), Emlyn Thomas (chairman), John Ivor Jones (dispute agent), Gwilym Evans, Bryn Bailey, Len Jones.

Left: A wet note issued by fireman Jimmy Thomas dated 18 July 1978 to Byron 'German' Davies. (He had a wet note written on a cog stick, he ascended the shaft in a minecar and they called him the colliery hooter). A wet note gives permission to a miner who had worked in wet conditions to travel the main haulage plane and to ascend the pit before the end of his working day with no deduction to his wages. Life underground, down in the bowels of the earth, was hazardous but coal-mining was a daily and regular feature for me all my working life. If asked to describe life underground I would say: 'It's not easy with the appalling conditions, roof breaking, timber creaking, stones falling, coal and stone dust rising, up to your knees in water, poor ventilation, using naked flame lamps and inadequate safety flame lamps giving insufficient light (about one candle light), sweat running, blood seething and, on some occasions, breath failing.' – yet this was the way the miner earned his bread and butter.

The 1984-1985 Miners Strike. The longest strike in South Wales and British mining history. Within a week every South Wales miner was on strike and the South Wales Coalfield was to be the most solid for the duration of the yearlong strike. In the quarter of a century prior to the strike, the area had suffered as catastrophic a decline as any area of the British Coalfield. Year ending March 1948 with a manpower of 108,000 produced 23,913,000tons and on 31 March 1984 with a manpower of 20,347 the estimated output due to the overtime ban was 6,720,000tons. Coal-mining in South Wales had declined and during the 1960s and early 1970s, when so many collieries were closed. The photograph includes: Harry Coombs (dispute agent), Alyn 'Boogie' Morgan, Ron 'Jampots' Williams, Emlyn Williams (NUM president), Garry Mathews, Doug Oliver.

Mardy Colliery underground link up with Tower Colliery on 14 May 1986 and they were only ½half an inch out of point! The photograph includes: Trevor Chapman (fireman) and Revd Norman Hadfield (ventilation officer). The colliery was owned by the Powell Duffryn Steam Coal Co. prior to nationalisation in 1947. Mardy No.3 and No.4 Colliery the last colliery in the Rhondda Valley was closed on Friday 21 December 1990 by British Coal.

Fernhill Colliery Blaenrhondda in 1969 – it stood at 804ft OD. At the head of the Rhondda Fawr, Ebenezer Lewis secured a mineral concession on the land on behalf of the owners J. Marychurch & Partners and the No.1 and No.2 Pits were sunk to the Six-Feet seam in 1871 and was then sold to Messrs Crowley, John and Oldroyd of Dewsbury who sank Nos 3, 4 and 5 in 1872. In 1877 they sold to George Watkinson & Sons. In 1893 George Watkinson & Sons bought the Blaenrhondda Colliery which was then absorbed into the Fernhill combine which was called Fernhill Collieries Ltd. They also drove the neighbouring Dunraven Levels. On 12 January 1872 the accident reports show that forty-eight-year-old engine man W. Thomas was killed by a rope and on 16 November 1872 the accident reports show that twenty-three-year-old collier William Thomas was killed by a fall of stone.

Fernhill Colliery Pit Bottom in the 1950s. In 1962, shafts Nos 1, 2 and 4 were filled in leaving Nos 3 and 5 for the link up with Tower. In 1964 Fernhill and Tower were 'linked' underground to form a single streamlined unit, employing 860 men that produced an annual tonnage of around 250,000tons. All the coal was taken by conveyor through to Tower colliery where it was washed and blended at the coal preparation plant, its coal at this time was semi-anthracite, used for domestic heating and for the manufacture of the popular smokeless fuel 'Phurnacite'. Fernhill Colliery was closed in March 1966 by the NCB.

Glenrhondda Colliery Blaencwm in 1940 was also known as the 'Hook and Eye'. The No.1 pit was opened in 1911 by the Glenavon Garw Colliery Co. and the No.2 pit was opened in 1921. The owners also worked a series of levels. In 1913 the manpower was 230, in 1954 with a manpower of 391 produced 76,679tons; in 1957 with a manpower of 404 produced 116,828tons.

Glenrhondda Colliery in 1948. An underground Jigger conveyor in a very unusual usage of a gate road conveyor taking the coal from a coalface belt conveyor. In 1957, with a manpower of 404, the colliery produced 116,828tons; in 1958, with a manpower of 392, it produced 97,387tons; in 1960, with a manpower of 403, it produced 82,767tons; and in 1961, with a manpower of 381, produced 76,788tons. Glenrhondda Colliery was closed in July 1966 by the NCB.

Graig Level Blaencwm in 1965. The mine was opened in 1858 by Thomas Jones. (A) is the tip that was at the mouth of the level, (B) is the remains of the dram incline and (C) is the bridge, which carried the dram road over the railway line and on to the washery screens of the Glenrhondda Colliery nearby. Graig Level closed the 1950s.

Left: Soviet Level during the 1926 strike. In June 1925 the coalowners announced that current wage contracts would end in one month's time. The miners' federation rejected the owners ultimatum and the TUC offered its support. By the end of July, it was clear the Government stood with the coalowners while the miners' federation had the backing of the TUC. Prime Minister Stanley Baldwin made an 'offer'. He said that the government would set up an inquiry into the entire situation and while that inquiry was sitting it would provide a subsidy to maintain miners wages at their current level. The proposal was made on 31 July 1925 and became known as 'Red Friday'. In early March 1926 the report was found in favour of the coalowners. The owners again issued an ultimatum on reducing wages. The miners executive committee rejected these demands and general secretary A.J. Cook coined the famous battle phrase 'Not a penny off the pay, not a minute on the day!' On 30 April the owners posted notices imposing a lock-out and on that day, the King signed a proclamation declaring Britain to be in a 'state of emergency'. At midnight on 3 May all production, all communications ground to a halt. Then suddenly, on 12 May the general strike was called off and the miners union was left to fight alone. They struggled on into the autumn. Then, towards the end of November 1926, miners around the country, exhausted, betrayed and deserted, resumed work in all the major coalfields with the exception of South Wales, Yorkshire and Durham who returned to work on 30 November. The lock-out had lasted for seven months. They went back to conditions imposed by the owners. Never in the history of the British trade union movement had there been such an industrial struggle. The Moscow Level at Blawncwm was acquired by the NCB from the Glenrhondda Garw Co. Ltd while in production in 1947.

Tydraw Colliery, Treherbert, in 1900. Locally known as the Dunraven Colliery was sunk in 1865 by Thomas Joseph of Aberdare on behalf of the Dunraven United Collieries Co. Ltd and went into liquidation in 1866. In 1872 the colliery was sold for £155,000 to Edmund Hanney Watts, William Milburn and Edward Stout and following many years of good production sold on to Cory Bros of Cardiff. The colliery was owned by the Powell Duffryn Steam Coal

Co. prior to nationalisation in 1947. In 1954 the seams worked were the Lower-Six-Feet, the Yard and the Five-Feet. In 1954 with a manpower of 383 produced 92,000tons and in 1958 with a manpower of 358 produced 52,766tons. Tydraw Colliery was closed in January 1959 by the NCB.

Lady Margaret Colliery, Treherbert, in 1911. The colliery was sunk in 1877 by the Marques of Bute and worked the Two-Feet-Nine, Four-Feet and the Six-Feet coal seams. The Blaenrhondda railway line was completed in 1894 and the Rhondda Tunnel with access to Swansea opened in 1889. With the coupling of the Taff Vale Railway and the Swansea Bay Railway, coal could be quickly transported to Cardiff and Swansea Docks. The Lady Margaret Colliery closed in 1909.

Bute Colliery, Treherbert, in 1885. The colliery was the first steam coal colliery to be sunk in the Rhondda Valley in September 1855 by William Southern Clarke, chief mining engineer to Lord Bute, for the trustees of the estate of Lord Bute. The coal was transported by horse drawn wagons to Gelligaled and loaded onto the first mineral train to Cardiff. In 1913 the manpower was 580 and in 1920 the manpower was 722. On 23 October 1868 the accident reports show that thirty-five-year-old collier J. Cox was killed by a fall of stone. On 27 January 1872 the accident reports show that fifty-three-year-old timberman T. Davis and twenty-two-year-old timberman J. Davis were killed while ascending the shaft when a dram fell down the pit and broke the rope. The Bute Colliery was closed in 1926 by the United National Collieries.

Ynysfaio Colliery, Ynyswen, in 1910. The colliery stood at 698ft OD. The photograph was taken on top of the pit (pit bank). The mineral property of 1,000 acres was purchased in 1854 by the Troedyrhiw Coal Co. and was sunk by James Thomas of Ynyshir and his partners, Mathew Cope of Cardiff and John Lewis of Aberdare. In 1874 the colliery output was around 36,000tons. On 29 June 1868 the accident reports show that fourteen-year-old doorboy J. Evans was killed by a journey of drams. The colliery was owned by the Powell Duffryn Steam Coal Co. prior to nationalisation. Ynysfaio Colliery was acquired by the NCB in 1947 and employed three men for pumping mine water.

Above: Tylacoch Colliery, Treorchy, in 1872. The colliery was sunk in 1854 by Messrs John Carr, Morrison & Co. On 23 January 1868 the accident reports show that thirty-five-year-old collier David Thomas and twenty-eight-year-old collier John Lewis was killed by an explosion. *Top right:* Tylacoch Colliery in 1866. The colliery was bought by United National Company in 1917. The photograph shows the pit in the progress of deepening the shaft. On 14 February 1872 the accident reports show that E. Davis labourer was killed by a truck passing over her. Tylacoch Colliery was closed in 1895. *Right:* Abergorki Colliery, Treorchy, in 1880. The colliery started production in 1865 and was sold to Burnyeat Brown & Co. in 1874 who sank the shafts into the steam coal seams and produced 50,000tons of coal in 1866. In 1913 the manpower was 1,926 and in 1920 the manpower was 1,800. In 1926 the colliery was sold to the Ocean Coal Co. On 13 June 1868 the accident reports show that eighteen-year-old collier David Richards was killed by a fall of roof. On 24 August 1872 the accident reports show that forty-one-year-old collier E. Kinsey was also killed by a fall of stone. The photograph shows women surface hauliers in 1880; their work also included greasing dram wheels and sheaves. Abergorki Colliery closed in April 1938.

The Park Colliery, Cwmparc, in 1918. Sinking began in 1864 by David Davies Co. In 1935 the Dare became part of the Powell Duffryn Steam Coal Co. prior to nationalisation in 1947 and acquired by the NCB in 1947. The coal seams worked were the Two-Feet-Nine, Lower-Six-Feet, Upper-Nine-Feet, Lower-Nine-Feet, Bute, Yard, Upper-Seven-Feet, Five-Feet and the Gellideg. In 1954 with the Dare Colliery and a manpower of 2,236 produced 336,000tons and in 1958 with a manpower of 2,003 produced 309,143tons. On 13 October 1868 the accident reports show that thirty-three-year-old collier David Richards was killed by a fall of stone and on 15 June 1872 the accident reports show that fifty-eight-year-old furnaceman William Davies was killed by being drawn up to the sheave. A person named William Thomas, who was insane, got into the engine-house and started the engine and could not stop it. The Park Colliery was closed in February 1966 by the NCB.

The Dare Colliery, Cwmparc, in 1919. Sinking began in 1864 by David Davies & Co: David Davies and Thomas Webb, Llandinam; Morgan Joseph, Ystradfechan; John Osborne Riches, Aberdare; Abraham Howell, Welshpool; and Ezra Roberts, Tenby. In 1877 the colliery was pur-chased by the Ocean Coal Co. Ltd and in 1890 employed 748 with an annual output of 184,000tons. In 1935 the Dare became part of the Powell Duffryn Steam Coal Co. and was acquired by the NCB in 1947. In 1955 the Dare was absorbed with the Park Colliery. In 1961 with the Park Colliery and a manpower of 1,867 produced 286,7000tons. On the 27 November 1873 the accident reports show that thirty-two-year-old rider David Bowen was killed by drams on the engine plane.

On 2 March 1874 the accident reports show that twenty-two-year-old collier J. Harris was killed by a fall of coal. The Dare Colliery was closed with the Park Colliery in February 1966 by the NCB.

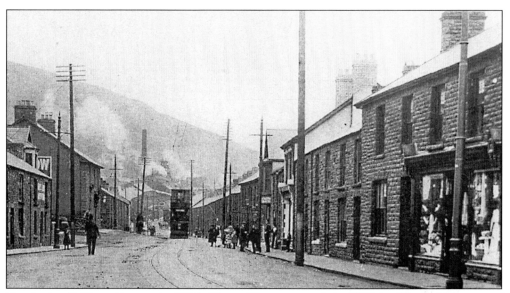

Tynybedw Colliery, Pentre, in 1909. The colliery was sunk in 1876 by Edmund Thomas of Maindy Hall and George Griffiths of Pontypridd and was locally known as the Swamp. On the left in the photograph is the Red Cow Hotel. Tynybedw Colliery closed in 1933.

Maindy Colliery, Pentre, in 1919. The colliery was sunk in 1864 by David Davies the founder of the Ocean Coal Co. This was his first venture into deep mining and they had just struck the Four-Feet coal seam before the finances ran out. In 1890 with a manpower of 1,220 men the colliery produced over 287,000tons of coal. In 1913 the manpower was only 215 men. On 30 May 1872 the accident reports show that twenty-five-year-old collier D. Davies was killed by a fall of stone. On 9 July 1872 the accident reports also show that forty-five-year-old collier J. Cakevell was killed by a fall of roof. Maindy Colliery was closed in April 1948 by the NCB.

Pentre Colliery, Pentre, in 1908. In 1857 the mineral rights were leased to Edward Curteis of, Llandaff, Cardiff, and developed the Pentre and Church levels. By 1864 the shafts of Pentre Colliery were sunk to the deeper seams. In 1867 the pit was owned by John Jones. In 1869 it was purchased by Cory Bros of Cardiff who developed the colliery and between 1874 and 1884 almost trebled the annual output from 59,000 to 159,000tons. On 24 February 1871 an explosion killed thirty-eight men and boys on 12 January 1874 the accident reports show that fifty-eight-year-old sinker W. Williams was killed by falling down the pit. Pentre Colliery closed in 1929.

Bodringallt Colliery, Ystrad, in 1910. The colliery was at 569ft OD and was sunk in 1864 by Warner Simpson & Co. and produced over 34,000tons of coal in its first year of operation. In 1890 the colliery was purchased by David Davis & Sons Ferndale and was called Ferndale No.3 Colliery. The colliery was later used for ventilation. The colliery was owned by the Powell Duffryn Steam Coal Co. prior to nationalisation in 1947. Bodringallt Colliery (Ferndale No.3) was closed with Ferndale No.1 and No.5 Colliery on 29 August 1959 by the NCB.

Gelli Colliery, Gelli, in 1960. The colliery was sunk in 1877 by Edmund Thomas. Five miners were killed when an explosion occurred in 1883. In 1884 the colliery was sold to the Cory Brothers of Cardiff who sold it to the Powell Duffryn Steam Coal Co. in 1935. The colliery was acquired by the NCB in 1947. The Five-Feet coal seam was worked. In 1955 with a manpower of 718, the colliery produced 166,261tons and in 1956, with a manpower of 698, it produced 150,796tons.

Gelli Colliery Winding Engine House in 1960. In 1957, with a manpower of 687, the colliery produced 134,861tons; in 1958, with a manpower of 654, it produced 138,564tons; in 1960, with a manpower of 605, it produced 89,460tons; and in 1961, with a manpower of 334, it produced 69,446tons. Gelli Colliery was closed in January 1962 by the NCB.

Llwynypia Colliery, Llwynypia, in 1918. It was situated at 455ft OD. Also known as the Glamorgan Colliery and the Scotch Colliery, it was opened from 1861 by the Glamorgan Coal Co. and in 1910 it was part of the Cambrian concern with No.1 Pit employing 1,712 men, the No.2 Pit, 1,539 and the No.5 Pit, 656. At 7.30p.m. on 25 January 1932 an explosion killed eleven miners, including two of the rescue team. A question of smoking was raised at the enquiry, but the cause of the explosion was never conclusively proved. The colliery was owned by the Powell Duffryn Steam Coal Co., ceased producing coal in 1932 and was used for pumping mine water.

Llwynypia Colliery By-Product Plant in 1918. The by-product plant produced bricks for the lining of the shafts during sinking and the surface colliery buildings. At its peak more than 10,000 bricks per day were produced – mostly by women. The bricks were dried undercover on iron floor plates heated by colliery waste gasses by means of under floor flues. The fireclay used for the bricks came from No.3 Pit, while working the No.3 coal seam. On 19 October 1872 the accident reports show that fifteen-year-old collier S. Emerson was killed by a fall of stone.

Cambrian Colliery Clydach Vale in 1910. In 1872 Samuel Thomas and J. Osborne Riches of the Cwmclydach Colliery Co. and Thomas Joseph of Aberdare sunk the No.1 shaft and in 1874 struck the Six-Feet coal seam at a depth of 400yds. The No.2 shaft was opened in 1875, and in 1899 the two pits produced over 1,000tons of coal per day. The No.3 shaft was sunk in 1889 and completed in 1891. In 1910 the manpower in No.1 Pit was 701, in No.2 Pit 1,498 and in No.3 Pit 1,855. On 7 August 1874 the accident reports show that collier J. Powell was killed by a fall of stone.

Cambrian Colliery Electric Generation Station in 1910. On 10 March 1905 an explosion killed thirty miners. At 1.00p.m. 17 May 1965 a further explosion also killed thirty-one miners. The colliery was owned by the Powell Duffryn Steam Coal Co. prior to nationalisation in 1947. Cambrian Colliery was closed on 24 September 1966 by the NCB.

May Day Strikers level Clydach Vale 1 May 1911. On 1 August 1910 the owners of the Ely Pit posted a lock-out. On 1 September 1910 the miners at the pit were locked-out and in dispute over an allowance to be paid for abnormal working condition in the Bute seam (2s 6d-a-ton on the ground had been demanded by the miners). By 1 November the 12,000 miners employed by the Cambrian concern were out on official strike. Work was resumed in October 1911 losing their local dispute; they had won the desired national movement to settle the wider question. The strike with all its bitter hardship and suffering had not been in vain.

Left: Fred Derick, formally of Glenview Clydach Vale in the 1920s. At the time of the photograph there were no pithead baths for the miners and this was a typical scene in the miners cottages after a days work at the colliery. Fred was employed at the Cambrian Colliery, Clydach Vale. In 1954 with a manpower of 1,996, the colliery produced 441,066tons; in 1955, with a manpower of 2,003, it produced 430,035tons; in 1956, with a manpower of 2,006, it produced 391,256tons; in 1957, with a manpower of 1,951, it produced 408,570tons; in 1958, with a manpower of 1,829, it produced 361,838tons; in 1960, with a manpower of 1,557, it produced 307,368tons; and in 1961, with a manpower of 1,549, it produced 315,687tons.

Blaenclydach Colliery, Blaenclydach, in 1938. The mine was opened in 1912 and was locally known as the Gorky Drift Mine. The photograph shows a group of miners at the end of the day shift enlightening from the spake (flat bottom man riding drams). At 7.00a.m. on 25 November 1941 the spake careered out of control – killing six men and badly injuring fifty-three miners. Gorky Drift Mine was closed in 1947 by the NCB.

Nantgwyn Colliery, Tonypandy, in 1910. The colliery was sunk in 1892 by the Naval Colliery Co. and in 1908 became part of the Cambrian concern. In 1910 the colliery employed 821 men and in 1913 employed 1,150 men. In 1928 the colliery ceased producing coal and was kept open for ventilation and pumping mine water. The colliery was owned by the Powell Duffryn Steam Coal Co. prior to nationalisation in 1947 and merged with the Naval Colliery in 1952. Nantgwyn Colliery was closed with the Naval Colliery in October 1958 by the NCB.

Naval Colliery, Penygraig, in 1910, situated 425ft OD. Locally known as the Pandy Pit, it was opened in 1875 by Moses Rowlands Jr, the chief partner in the Naval Colliery Co. The Anthony Pit was opened in 1910. In 1913 the colliery employed 850 and in 1947 employed 808 men. In 1954, with a manpower of 714, it produced 127,000tons; in 1955, with a manpower of 735, it produced 137,684tons; in 1956, with a manpower of 717, it produced 122,417tons; and in 1957, with a manpower of 437, it produced 90,485tons. On 13 February 1872 the accident reports show that forty-eight-year-old collier W. Samuel was killed by a fall of roof. On 28 November 1873 the accident reports also show that twenty-three-year-old collier John Jones was killed by a fall of roof. The colliery was owned by the Powell Duffryn Steam Coal Co. prior to nationalisation in 1947. Naval Colliery was closed with the Nantgwyn Colliery in October 1958 by the NCB.

The Naval Colliery explosion of 10 December 1880 at 1:15a.m., when 101 men and boys lost their lives. This photograph of the victims was taken following the explosion. On 27 January 1884 another explosion claimed the lives of eleven men and a further three belonging to the rescue team were suffocated while exploring after the explosion. Those who died were: Thomas Davies (46), Solomon Edwards (42), John Escott (27), John Heycock (42), John Heycock Jr (19), Oliver John (33), David Jones (52), Thomas Lewis (34), Fred Nugent (44), John Price (43), James Seville (49), Daniel Thomas (35), Edward Watkins (35), William Williams (61).

Ely Colliery, Penygraig, in 1920. The colliery was sunk in 1892 by the Naval Colliery Co. In 1910 a dispute which had serious consequences throughout the South Wales Coalfield for many years when the trouble began over the management offer of a piece rate for the new Bute coal seam which had been recently opened. The miners demanded more money because the seam was difficult to work. On 1 September 1910 the owners locked out not only the miners in dispute but also all the workmen employed at the colliery, a total of 950 men. On 1 November following a ballot, the South Wales Miners Federation called out the 12,000 miners employed by the Cambrian concern. There was great bitterness in the area, when it became known that the owners employed black-leg labour to keep the pumps and ventilation going at the Glamorgan Colliery, Llwynypia. This resulted in riots between police and miners. The strike continued until the autumn of 1911 when hardship and misery forced the miners to accept the coalowners offer. In 1913 the colliery employed 650 men. The colliery was owned by the Powell Duffryn Steam Coal Co. prior to nationalisation in 1947. Ely Colliery was closed in October 1958 by the NCB.

Dinas Middle Colliery, Dinas, in the 1880s. The colliery was situated at 382ft OD. In 1809 Walter Coffin bought Dinas Uchaf Farm to prospect for coal on the estate. His first level was opened to the Rhondda No.1 seam, which was difficult to work, and the coal was of poor quality. He then opened another level to the Rhondda No.2 coal seam and the coal was of good quality. In 1810 and 1811 he leased further mineral rights and in 1812 sank the Dinas Lower Colliery to the Rhondda No.3 seam, the first deep mine in the Rhondda Valley known as Coffins Coal. The Dinas Middle Colliery was sunk in 1832 by Walter Coffin. In 1886 a further shaft was opened by Daniel Thomas. On 1 January 1844 an explosion killed twelve men and boys and was the first major explosion in the Rhondda Valley. On 13 January 1879 a further explosion killed sixty-three men and boys. Dinas Colliery closed in 1893.

Dinas Mines Rescue Team in 1912. Dinas Mines Rescue Station was opened on the 27 June 1912 through a visit of King George V and Queen Mary. The rescue station in situated 200yds from the first shaft sunk in the Rhondda Valley by Walter Coffin. The building was built by contractors Messrs Niblett & Davies of Cardiff at a cost of £3,448 17s 3d.

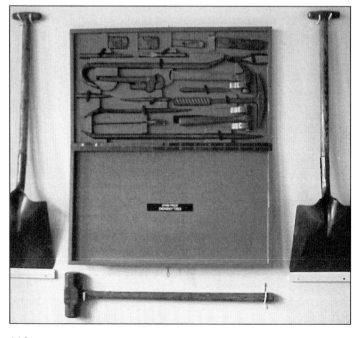

Dinas Mines Rescue Station emergency tools are made of non-ferrous (non-sparking) metal. The rescue station continues to serve Tower, Betws, Aberpergwm, Pentreclwydau South Mine, five small mines, the Forest of Dean and the West Country stone mines. The station Duty Room is manned daily and is able to turnout immediately at least one team of rescue men fully equipped with a rescue officer. The eighteen members of the rescue team and their families live in close proximity of the rescue station.

Output of coal from the Rhondda Valley Collieries 1914 to 1918

Year	Rhondda Valley	South Wales Collieries
1914	9,107,521 tons	53,880,000 tons
1915	7,958,731 tons	50,435,000 tons
1916	7,595,106 tons	52,081,000 tons
1917	8,667,209 tons	48,508,000 tons
1918	8,345,984 tons	46,717,000 tons

The Fernhill, Tydraw, Glenrhondda, Parc and Dare, Gelli, Cambrian, Naval, National and Lewis Merthyr Collieries were in the No.3 Rhondda Area of the South Western division of the NCB, an area which extended from Fernhill to Cwm, between Pontypridd and Llantrisant and from the Cambrian Collieries to Lady Windsor, Ynysybwl. Northward of the National Colliery Wattstown, the Collieries of Tylorstown No.8 and No.9, Ferndale No.1 and No.5 and the Mardy Collieries in the Rhondda Fach were in the No.4 Aberdare area.

The following are the colliery output of coal for the year 1957 and also giving a total output for that year of 2,380,201 tons.

Lewis Merthyr	217,569 tons
National	152,281 tons
Tylorstown No.9	164,097 tons
Ferndale No.1 and No.5	128,564 tons
Mardy	206,184 tons
Fernhill	263,029 tons
Glenrhondda	116,828 tons
Tydraw	74,656 tons
Parc & Dare	423,077 tons
Gelli	134,861 tons
Cambrian	408,570 tons
Naval	90,485 tons
Total	**2,380,201 tons**

The nerve centres of Rhondda mining were the headquarters of No.3 Area at Llwyncelyn Porth and the No.4 area at Aberaman in the Cynon Valley. New prospects were opening out in Rhondda coal mining. Since 1947, for the first time in the history of the South Wales Coalfield, mining the whole mineral basin as one unit had become possible, so that large-scale constructive improvements could be embarked upon. Small, uneconomic pits were being closed, ageing ones had been overhauled and provided with a new lease of life, and new, vast, imaginative mining projects were under way to ensure employment for men in collieries where reserves of coal were approaching exhaustion. Miners enjoyed pithead baths, ambulance centres, canteens and other amenities, and recruits were given the technical advantage of a sixteen-week training course at the Rhondda Area Training Centre at Wattstown. In this respect, the NCB had consolidated the pioneering plans of Lord Davies, chairman of Ocean and Wilson's Ltd, the one outstanding philanthropist among Rhondda Coalowners in the inter-war years.

Coal-mining comes to an end in the Rhondda Valley

With the nationalisation of the coal industry on 1 January 1947 came the promise of a new era of prosperity, particularly within the traditional strongholds of the industry such as South Wales. However, it became apparent that due to the nature of the geological faulting found in many areas of the coalfield, modern mining methods using the most modern of coal cutting equipment would not be possible. Accordingly, the NCB declared such areas economically unviable. Thus the arrival of the 1950s saw the coal board, despite striving to maintain high levels of production and regular employment, having to close collieries. Too soon the availability of cheap foreign imports, coupled with the introduction of oil and nuclear-powered electric generating stations were also to drastically affect the fortunes of the industry. Such a rapid decline in demand for home produced coal inevitably led to a further downward spiral in production and thus even more pit closures. Staggering from one crisis to another the already ailing industry was dealt a further blow with the commercial exploitation of North Sea Gas. The availability of this seemingly endless supply of fuel resulted in major losses of markets both in the domestic and industrial sectors.

Bowing to intense economic pressures the NCB continued to wield the axe. The Mineworkers Union were soon left in little doubt that these closures would result in over fifty per cent job losses.

For the displaced miners, dole and poverty once again, but for the old owners of these collieries, compensation and interest beyond the value of the pits they owned, which the NCB will continue to pay although the pits may be closed.

During the 1960s seventy-four collieries in the South Wales Coalfield stopped production and as the decade drew to a close, there came an increased militancy. Throughout November 1971, a rash of unofficial strikes over pay disputes caused great unrest in the Welsh mining communities. This industrial action brought matters to a head and a strike was called on the 9 January 1972. The national strike, the first since 1926, resulted in the whole of the South Wales Coalfield being brought to a standstill. It was to be almost two months before coal was again raised but the dispute, which had a devastating effect on British industry, saw the miners return to work as victors. To some, it was in some small way a vindication of their fathers and grandfathers who suffered such a humiliating defeat forty-six years earlier. The strike had shown that despite the increased use of oil and nuclear power as alternative energy sources, the nation's prosperity still relied heavily on coal. This knowledge won a temporary reprieve for those pits earmarked for closure and underlined the miners industrial might. Further unrest two years later again saw the union locked in a dispute, which ultimately brought down the Heath Government. However, by the end of the decade the tide began to turn with the NCB again sanctioning further cuts. Seeing confrontation as the only means to halt what they regarded as the destruction of an industry, the miners once more resorted to industrial action.

The strike of 1984 resulted in one of the longest and most acrimonious disputes ever to affect the mining industry. In its wake came the inevitable hardship and distress, which for many people rekindled memories of 1926. Locked in battle with an intransigent Thatcher Government the miners were beaten after a struggle which lasted over eleven months and which eventually saw a split in their ranks, the miners finally surrendered and returned to work. Soon after, the NCB implemented a plan of relentless pit closures, which saw the spectre of unemployment hang menacingly over the valley communities of South Wales. Even in decline it seemed, coal still brought despair to the majority of those who lived and worked in its shadow.

Such statistics underline the fact that nowhere in Britain has the decline in the coal industry been so keenly felt as in the South Wales Coalfield and especially the Rhondda Valley. Successive governments have often, without due consideration to the consequences to local communities, resorted to a programme of wholesale closure. The results of such politically orientated decisions came to threaten the very existence of an industry and the valley communities, which had for more than a century been totally dependent upon it. Today, those new industries, which are to be found in the valleys of South Wales have, despite claims to the contrary, often failed to provide local employment on a scale comparable with the coal industry. Thus, some would regard its decline with regret. However, perhaps many more view the loss of jobs as a small price to pay for an end to the terrible toll of human life, the suffering and the desecration of a once beautiful landscape, which were hallmarks of an era when coal was king.

There was always tremendous courage and staunch camaraderie with the South Wales miners in the deep, fiery and dangerous pits. 241 collieries closed in South Wales from 1921 to 1936. During the 1960s seventy-four collieries in the South Wales Coalfield stopped production. Mardy the last deep mine in the Rhondda Valley closed on Friday 21 December 1990.

Three

The Ely Valley in the South Wales Coalfield

Among the colliery undertakings in the South Wales Coalfield was that of the Powell Duffryn Steam Coal Co. Ltd, in fact it may be said that it was one of the largest, most modern and best equipped in the world at the time. In 1840 Thomas Powell commenced sinking a pit at Tir Ffounder near Aberdare. Developments rapidly followed and in less than a quarter of a century he had steam coal collieries, which were then known as Cwmdare, Abernant-y-Groes, Abergwawr, Tir Ffounder, Middle Duffryn and Cwm Pennar in the Cynon Valley. In 1864 Thomas Powell disposed of the whole of these properties to the Powell Duffryn Steam Coal Co. Ltd. The capital of the new concerns was £5m. In 1866 the High Duffryn Colliery was acquired and in the same year Mr Crawshay Bailey sold the company the Aberaman estate, including the Aberaman Ironworks and collieries at Aberaman and Treaman and in view of this purchase it was decided to make Aberaman the headquarters of the company. Before the end of 1866, the company's undertakings were further extended by the acquisition of Cwmneol and Fforchaman Collieries from the United Merthyr Collieries Co.

From its inception, Powell Duffryn coal, have always ranked amongst the highest class of Welsh Steam Coal. In the early 1870s the British admiralty experimented with the idea of discovering coal suitable for the Navy and subject all descriptions of coal to prolonged test and it was as a result of these tests that Welsh coal incontestably proved their superiority for Naval purposes. The company became familiarly known as the PDs.

In 1920 the PDs acquired the 4,000 acres in the Llantrisant area, the lower end of the Ely Valley. *South Wales Collieries Vol.I* photographs include: PDs Collieries in the Cynon, Rhondda and the Ely Valleys.

Year 1947

Tower	In production	Tylorstown Nos 8 & 9	In production
Cwmdu Uchaf Level	Closed	Ferndale Nos 1 & 5	In production
Blaenant	Closed	Ferndale Nos 2 & 4	Closed
Lletyshenkin	Closed	Mardy Nos 1 & 2	Closed
Upper Duffryn	Closed	Mardy Nos 3 & 4	Not in production
Fforchaman	In production	Tydraw	In production
Abergwawr	Closed	Ynysfeio	Not in production
Aberaman	In production	Park and Dare	In production
Deep Duffryn	In production	Gelli	In production
Lower Duffryn	Not in production	Bodringallt	Not in production
Penrikyber	In production	Glamorgan	Not in production
Abercynon	In production	Nantgwyn	Not in production
Albion	In production	Cambrian	In production
Penrhiw	Not in production	Naval	In production
Maritime	In production	Ely	In production
Tŷ mawr	In production	Cilely	In production
Lewis Merthyr	In production	Britannic	In production
Lady Lewis	In production	Cwm	In production
Tylorstown Nos 6 & 7	Not production	Llantrisant	Closed

Cilely Colliery, Tonyrefail, in 1925. The No.1 shaft was known as the Peggy Pit, the No.2 known as the Water Pit and was sunk between 1872 and 1874 by D. Davis & Sons of Blaengwawr to the Rhondda No.3 coal seam at a depth of 40yds. The shafts were later deepened to the steam coal seams known as the lower measures. No.3 the Jubilee Pit was sunk in 1909 to 1912. On the left in the photograph is the No.3 Jubilee Pit, in the middle is the No.2 Water Pit and in the background of its headgear is the No.1 Peggy Pit. On 13 July 1875 the accident reports show that twenty-three-year-old sinker H. Davies and twenty-five-year-old sinker were killed by a trolley falling down the shaft upon them.

Cilely Colliery Winding Sheave in 1914. The winding wheel is either being drawn up the headstock or has just been lowered for changing. The block and tackle lifting gear is shown attached to the wheel.

Cilely Colliery Surface Workers in 1910. The man second row from back, second left, is Tom Davies known as 'Twmi gwaith' (Tommy work) who allegedly almost lived at work. Seams worked were the Rhondda No.3, Four-Feet, Red Vein and the Jubilee.

Cilely Colliery No.2 the Water Pit Winding Engine in 1930. No.2 was always referred as the water pit because for many years only water was pumped and wound in tanks from the No.2 shaft. Cilely Colliery was closed in October 1950 by the NCB.

Cilely Colliery No.1, Peggy Pit Bottom in 1930. On the left in the photograph holding a safety oil lamp is Mr Hubert Clark head surveyor of the colliery. In 1913 the colliery manpower was 584, in 1920 the manpower was 700 and in 1947 the manpower was 569. The colliery was owned by the Powell Duffryn Steam Coal Co, prior to nationalisation in 1947.

Rhiwgarn Level, Tonyrefail, also known as Cilely Level, in 1900. The mine was opened in 1885 and belonged to the Cilely Colliery they also had the same senior officials. The seam of coal worked was the Rhondda No.2. The man in the photograph is said to be Mr W.J. Rees (undermanager) and his certificate number was 2,880 second class.

Caerlan Level, Tonyrefail, in 1905. The dram of coal was being brought from the levels and was taken across Barn Hill, Penrhiwfer, to a place locally known as Brown Pitch, where the railway sidings were located near Gelligron Farm. The haulier is believed to be of the Sutton family of Williamstown and the boy is an assistant haulier.

Hafod Level, Tonyrefail, in 1965. The entrance was situated on Gelligron land opposite Collenna drift mine. The mine worked the Hafod, Rhondda No.1 and Rhondda No.2 coal seams.

Left: Collenna Drift Mine, Tonyrefail, in 1900. The mine was opened in 1878 by Glamorgan Coal Co. who worked the Rhondda No.2, the Rhondda No.3 and Hafod coal seams. The angle of the main drift was 51° (approximately 44in to the yard). Traffic men (journey attendants) at work. Collenna Drift mine closed in 1912. *Right:* Mr and Mrs Acreman and family at the rear of Fountain Row in the early 1930s.

Glyn Drift Mine, Tonyrefail, in 1901. The mine was opened in 1878 and worked the Rhondda No.2, Rhondda No.3 and the Forest Fach housecoal seams. Situated on the Glyn Mountain, the main drift dipped at 1ft to 2ft 6in. The mine employed over 400 men and boys at its peak of production. The coal was worked by the old tophole method. This method was, in some ways a forerunner of the horizon technique of mining. Naked lights were used in the mine. Glyn Drift Mine closed in 1903.

Tylchafach Drift Mine, Nantymelin Tonyrefail, in 1910. The mine was opened in 1872 by Mr Hugh Begg, manager at the Dinas Isaf Pit, upper Ely Valley. The photograph includes: William 'Bill Kitty' Middleton, Nat Evans and John 'Johnnie Kneeldown' Lloyd. Acquired by Welsh Navigation Steam Coal Co. in 1912/1913 and worked in conjunction with Coedely Colliery who washed and screened the coal. The Tydu coal seam was worked at a thickness of 2ft 6in to 6ft and was highly bituminous and very sulphury. The floor of the seam was mostly good quality fire clay and was used for brick making at Coedely. The roof of the seam was hard sandstone and was mined extensively for building many of the surface buildings in the area. Best example of 'Peg and Ball' naked flame lights, known as Myglyd (smokey). Tylchafach Drift Mine closed in 1930.

Left: David Ellis who lived at Penrhiwfer, Tonyrefail, worked at the local collieries and was known as Ellis 'Bandy' from the shape of his legs *Right:* Etna Colliery, Gilfach Goch, in 1911. Locally known as Locks Level and Dyllas Isaf. The mine was owned by Mr Lock a grocer from Williamstown and worked the Rhondda No.2 seam. The level was inundated with a rush of water at 9.00a.m. on 19 March 1911, which drowned Evan Lewis and his fourteen-year-old son, Thomas John Lewis. The volume of water also partly destroyed the bank and buildings of the railway station.

119

Scotch Level Gilfach Goch in the Cwm Ogwr Valley in 1900. The Scotch level was opened by the Glamorgan Coal Co. in 1878 and worked the Rhondda No.2 and the Rhondda No.3 seams. The collier is undercutting the coal with a mandrel and a naked candlelight is in use. Scotch Level closed in 1964.

Dinas Main Colliery, Gilfach Goch, in 1910. The colliery was situated at 831ft OD, it was sunk in 1864 by Christmas Evans, son of Evan Evans of Six Bells. On 12 December 1907 an explosion killed seven men and the pit was closed and never worked again. Naked flame lights were in use at the time. During its existence the pit was acquired and became part of the larger Britannic Colliery complex.

Britannic Merthyr Colliery, Gilfach Goch, in 1900. The colliery was 782ft OD, it was sunk in 1895 by Britannic Coal Co. The seams worked were the Four-Feet, Six-Feet, Nine-Feet, Seven-Feet, Pentre, Bute, Yard and the Gellideg. The colliery was owned by the Powell Duffryn Steam Coal Co. prior to nationalisation in 1947. Britannic Merthyr Colliery was closed on 30 January 1960 by the NCB.

Britannic Colliery, Mavor & Coulson Undercutter in 1949. In 1954, with a manpower of 694, it produced 156,732tons; in 1955, with a manpower of 690, it produced 147,929tons; in 1956, with a manpower of 709, it produced 173,869tons; in 1957, with a manpower of 602, it produced 103,626tons; in 1958, with a manpower of 671, it produced 245,597tons; in 1960, with a manpower of 586, it produced 188,000tons; and in 1961, with a manpower of 598, produce 168,868tons.

Britannic Colliery, Anderson Boyes, Shearer Loader in 1955. On 1 October 1901 the accident reports show that forty-four-year-old lamp carrier Isaac Williams was killed by entering a moving cage. On 11 October 1910 the accident reports show that Sammy Price, assistant manager, was suffocated by methane gas, on the 13 October 1901 the accident reports show that twenty-three-year old collier Joe Bonner was killed by a large roof fall.

Britannic Colliery Transfer Point in 1955. On 27 November 1903 the accident reports show that thirty-five-year-old timberman W.E. Pugh was run over by drams leaving a parting. On 20 October 1910 the accident reports also show that thirty-five-year-old fireman R.L Davies was killed while he was examining repairs in a horse road. A repairer who knocked out a post under a broken collar caused a large fall of roof.

Coedely Colliery, Coedely, in 1918. The colliery was opened in 1901 by D. Davis & Sons, of Blaengwawr, who worked the Rhondda No.2 and the Rhondda No.3 seams. By 1921 was in the hands of the Welsh Navigation Steam Coal Co. Ltd. The colliery was owned by the Powell Duffryn Steam Coal Co. prior to nationalisation in 1947. When the colliery was merged with the Cwm Colliery by the NCB it became the largest unit in South Wales. In 1947 the coal seams worked were the Pentre No.1 and the Lower Pentre No.2. In 1954, with a manpower of 836, the colliery produced 221,498tons; in 1955, with a manpower of 888, it produced 171,165tons; and in 1956, with a manpower of 854, it produced 145,581tons.

Coedely Colliery Conveyor Track in the Rhondda No.3 coal seam in 1939 showing the amount of squeeze (roof pressure on the coalface). The naked flame safety oil lamp was approximately 10in high and the roof would have lowered from a full 3ft to what appears to be near 15-18in. The jigger conveyors were in use at this time. In 1957, with a manpower of 823, the colliery produced 193,137tons; in 1958, with a manpower of 856, it produced 182,747tons; in 1960, with a manpower of 825, it produced 162,089tons; and in 1961, with a manpower of 925, it produced 183,739tons. Coedely Colliery was closed in 1985 by the NCB.

Cwm Colliery, Beddau, in 1913. The colliery, sunk in 1909 by the Great Western Colliery Co. Ltd, was known as the Mildred and Margaret Pits and was merged with Coedely Colliery in 1956. The colliery was owned by the Powell Duffryn Steam Coal Co. prior to nationalisation in 1947. In 1954, with a manpower of 1,346, the colliery produced 263,974 tons; in 1955, with a manpower of 1,303, it produced 256,187tons; in 1956, with a manpower of 1,381, it produced 298,871tons; in 1957, with a manpower of 1,466, it produced 298,871tons; in 1958, with a manpower of 1,457, produced 270,291tons; in 1960, with a manpower of 1,740, produced 324,790tons; and in 1961, with a manpower of 1,463, produced 300,275tons. Cwm Colliery was closed on 28 November 1986 by the NCB.

Cwm Colliery Pit Bottom in 1981. The seams worked at Cwm/Coedely in 1981 were the Six-Feet and the Five-Feet. With coalface lengths between 130yds and 250yds. On 5 April 1949 one miner died and fifteen were injured when gas was ignited by shot-firing.

Llantrisant Colliery, Ynysmaerdy, in 1925. The pit was first known as New Duffryn. The colliery was sunk by Powell Duffryn Steam Coal Co. in 1923. The seams worked were the Rhondda No.2 and the Rhondda No.3. Llantrisant Colliery ceased production in 1941.

The Llantrisant Colliery explosion at No.2 Shaft. At 1.45p.m. on 2 June 1941 an explosion killed four men, they were: John Gregor (agent/manager), Noab Fletcher (winding engineman), David Thomas (switch board attendant) and Ernest Evans (banksman). Most of the surface buildings and pithead was destroyed.

Left: Llantrisant Colliery in 1936. The collier on the puncher (pneumatic pick, one of the causes of vibration white finger) is Tom Neat with his son also named Tom Neat. *Right:* three-year-old Kieron Montague and 'Butty' Martin Roderick in 1987. On 1 January 1947 the coming of nationalisation brought the promise of a new era of prosperity to the villages. Such optimism was sadly never realised. Within a few short years pit closures began to spread throughout the length and breadth of the South Wales Coalfield. The Mineworkers Union was soon left in little doubt that these closures would result in job losses. There would be no future in mining for these young lads. Mardy No.3 and No.4, the last deep mine in the Rhondda Valley, closed on Friday 21 December 1990.

David 'Dai Craith' Jones a Valley Miner
You might say that Dai Craith had a physiognomy, which betrayed his nature, while his voice revealed it. His rugged features, flattened nose with a stitch scar (craith) right across it, deep sunk eyes, thin lips, almost cauliflower ears, all betoken the boxer.

Yet his low voice was gentle and musical. As he spoke the impression of the pugilist faded and the more genuine impression of a quiet, retiring, reliable personality replaced it. Imaging the lilting Welsh voice talking to you.

He was born in 1888, of a Welsh family with a tradition of four generations. He was twelfth in a family of fourteen.

He left school at thirteen but was sent back and compelled to stay until he'd passed the Labour Examination two months later. Back at the colliery, he went underground as a fireman's assistant. After a month he moved to a job on the endless haulage. He had to be at his post $2\frac{1}{2}$ miles from the pit bottom at 6.00a.m., which meant getting up at four o'clock.

Back home at 430p.m. he often fell straight asleep in a chair still in his pit black clothes, unless he had a date, when he would compete with his father and brothers in the rush to be in the old tin bath in front of the fire.

Coalmining almost came to an end in the South Wales Valleys with over Seventy Collieries closing from 1947 to 1990.

With the nationalisation of the coal industry on the 1 January 1947 came the promise of a new era of prosperity, particularly within the traditional strongholds of the industry such as South Wales. However, it became apparent that due to the nature of the geological faulting found in many areas of the coalfield, modern mining methods using the most modern of coal cutting equipment would not be possible. Accordingly, the NCB declared such areas economically unviable. Thus the arrival of the 1950s saw the coal board, despite striving to maintain high levels of production and regular employment, having to close collieries. Too soon the availability of cheap foreign imports, coupled with the introduction of oil and nuclear powered electric generating stations were also to drastically affect the fortunes of the industry. Such a rapid decline in demand for home produced coal inevitably led to a further downward spiral in production and thus even more pit closures. Staggering from one crisis to another the already ailing industry was dealt a further blow with the commercial exploitation of North Sea Gas. The availability of this seemingly endless supply of fuel resulted in major losses of markets both in the domestic and industrial sectors.

Bowing to intense economic pressures the NCB continued to wield the axe.

Within a few short years pit closures began to spread throughout the length and breadth of the South Wales Coalfield. The Mineworkers Union were soon left in little doubt that these closures would result in over fifty per cent job losses.

During the 1960s seventy-four collieries in the South Wales Coalfield stopped production and more cuts came at the end of the 1970s. Following the strike of 1984/85 the NCB implemented a plan of relentless pit closures, which saw the spectre of unemployment hang menacingly over the valley communities of South Wales. Even in decline it seemed, coal still brought despair to the majority of those who lived and worked in its shadow.

Such statistics underline the fact that nowhere in Britain has the decline in the coal industry been so keenly felt as in The Cynon Valley, the Rhondda Valley and the Ely Valley.

Mardy the last colliery in the Rhondda Valley closed on Friday 21 December 1990. Tower Colliery is the only remaining deep mine in the Cynon Valley. November 2001.

Heritage and Culture of the Valleys

Strange though it may seem, the discovery of a fossil fuel deep within the earth's core has borne a unique wealth of culture to the entwining valleys and shaped the nature of modern South Wales.

The black coal heaps (tips) may have been removed, but the heritage and culture of the coal communities lives on in the terraced house, Italian Cafes, Theatres and Museums of the region.

However, whilst the communities of the South Wales Valleys are proud of their history, the latter half of this century has generally dictated a more modern approach to industry and commerce. Leisure and tourism are on the increase and visitors to the region can now enjoy a delightful mix of old interspersed with new as dedicated attractions provide a telling portrait of the legacy of coal and its role in the new millennium.

With coal came the upsurge of religion and the establishment of the Arts. The hymn singing legacy of the Welsh Chapels gave rise to the renowned Welsh Male Voice Choirs and the Valleys fostered the development of performers such as Tom Jones and actors Glyn and Donald Houston and Sir Stanley Baker.

The colliery tips have been landscaped, nature has returned to the valleys and has carved a beautiful backdrop of rolling hills, vales, mountains and rich meadows. The area is abundant with natural wildlife, where fish swim lazily in the clear water of the rivers where forty-six different kinds of wild flowers naturally grow in its banks.

Carwriaeth

Y tân yn oeri'n araf
A'r lluniau wedi ffoi;
Y fodrwy wedi lacio,
A'r bys yn dal i'w throi.

Y llestri ar fwrdd y gegin
A'r slippers dan y stôl,
Yn disgwyl trigain mlynedd
I ddod trwy'r drws yn ôl.

The Miner's Wife

In fire's dying embers
No pictures now remain,
The ring is slack on the finger,
It turns again and again.

Dishes are set on the table,
Slippers' neath the stool on the floor
Awaiting sixty years to return
And walk right in through the door.

Lamp Y Glowr

Cawsant ef, a'i lamp a'r fandrel
A heb arno farc na chlwy'
Draw yn nos y talcen eithaf
Lle na chanai 'deryn mwy.

Yn nhywyllwch yr unigedd
Y mae lamp nas gwelwn ni,
O dan liain yr anwylo
Mae'n 'Aladdin' iddi hi.

The Miner's Lamp

He was found with lamp and mandrel
And without a wound or mark
In the blackness of the coalface
- No bird sang there in the dark.

In his wife's world – dark and lonely
There's a lamp we cannot see,
Magic 'neath her soft caresses
- Aladdin's lamp of memory.

Glyn James
Hon. Alderman and former Lord Mayor of the Rhondda Valley

A Fourth Selection
for the
Third Millennium